GEEK LUST

POP CULTURE, GADGETS, AND OTHER DESIRES
OF THE LIKEABLE MODERN GEEK

ALEX LANGLEY

Published by

Krause Publications, a division of F+W Media, Inc.
700 East State Street • Iola, WI 54990-0001
715-445-2214 • 888-457-2873
www.krausebooks.com

To order books or other products call toll-free 1-800-258-0929
or visit us online at www.krausebooks.com

Cover photo: Liz Lemon (Tina Fey) from *30 Rock*. Copyright 2012
NBCUniversal Media, LLC/Getty Images.
Back cover: Princess Leia (Carrie Fisher)—Lucasfilm/20th Century Fox/Heritage Auctions.

Information on photos inside the book, along with copyright credits, starts on Page 231.

ISBN-13: 978-1-4402-3860-4
ISBN-10: 1-4402-3860-X

Edited by Kristine Manty
Cover Design by Nicole MacMartin
Designed by Nicole MacMartin

Printed in the United States of America

> To Katrina,
> You take the robots, I'll take the ninjas.
> Ready?

Special Thanks

Special thanks to Katrina Hill, Alan Kistler, S.G. Browne, Jessica Mills, Travis Langley, and Annie Neugebauer for contributing their wise words to my book. You guys rock my butt off.

Thanks to Nicholas, Mom, and Dad for being awesome and helping me up grow in an awesome-rich environment.

Thanks to my extended family for encouraging me to do what I do even if you don't always understand what I do.

Thanks to my friends, my second family, who've helped keep me laughing and keep me going. Give yourselves a pat on the back and a French kiss for me.

Thanks to the Denton North Branch Writer's Critique Group for putting up with my shenanigans as I try to better myself as a professional word-maker and keyboard smasher.

Thanks to the OC Remix community for giving me such amazing music to listen to while working on my many, many projects.

Thanks to all the amazing writers, thinkers, and content creators listed in this book. Without your contributions, I wouldn't be the writer I am today.

Contents

87 | **MOVIES:** Books for Your Eyes and Earholes

185 | **BOOKS:** Take a Look, It's in a Book

230 | **EPILOGUE:** I Dream of Electric Sheep. Also, of Spider-Man Giving Me a Chemistry Test While I'm Naked

231 | **PHOTO CREDITS**

233 | **INDEX**

Introduction

Geek Passion: Burning Like 1.21 Giga-Suns

Geeks and lust are two words that, traditionally, haven't really gone together. But the meanings of both words have changed. "Geek" is no longer a term to refer to isolated, intelligent people or sideshow attractions,[1] and "Lust" no longer just means having a feeling of teh bonerz for someone else. No, these two terms have one powerful, common factor: passion. Geeks are passionate about what we do; we don't merely enjoy these things, we *lust* after them. Our geekery is a fire that consumes every fiber of our beings. Computer geeks obsess over the latest innovations in technology, movie geeks can't wait to see how the next *Star Wars* flick turns out, and cereal geeks go inexplicably ballistic for new kinds of Cap 'N Crunch.

I've devoted this book to as many different areas of geekdom as I could cram into it. In these pages you'll find:

- Discussions of storytelling mediums, such as movies, TV shows, and comic books, which excite the mind and stimulate the intellect.
- Thoughts on our relaxing and distracting hobbies of playing video games and surfing the internet.
- Musings on where geeks will take us in the future: will physics geeks unlock the secret to time travel and reduce the universe to a big ball of wibbly wobbly, timey wimey stuff? Will robotics geeks figure out a way to transfer a person's consciousness into a machine and render them immortal? Will candy geeks figure out how many licks it does take to get to the Tootsie Roll center of a Tootsie Pop?

Objects of a geek's lust can be as varied as the colors of the Power Rangers. I, myself, am obsessed with story-telling, comedy, and video games, in that order; without these things I'd feel incomplete. If I were stuck on a desert island, I would probably spend my days writing stories, my evenings telling jokes to the coconuts, and my nights playing video games using sticks and sand. While lust, in the traditional sense, is something we need and desire, Geek Lust is something we can't live without.

---

[1] The original meaning of the word geek refers to circus freaks, including people who bit the heads off of chickens. True story.

Chapter 1

Science Rules

The theme song to *Bill Nye the Science Guy* says it so well: science rules. As do math, history, literature—pretty much anything we can study and better ourselves with. Just think of where the world would be without academically minded geeks studying up and forging a better tomorrow. On second thought, don't think about that world because it sucks and is stupid. Instead look to the present and to the future, and marvel at all the awesomeness brought to us by science and academia.

Dr. Albert Einstein writes out an equation for the density of the Milky Way—the galaxy, not the candy bar—at the Carnegie Institute on Jan. 14, 1931.

Speculative Science: I'd Like Some Bionic Arms with a Side of Fries

The advancement of the human condition isn't always about looking at what we have, it's about looking at what we don't have—that's called speculative science, baby. The Wright Brothers weren't born with wings, so they built the world's first successful airplane. Alexander Graham Bell didn't want to wander door-to-door to see which of his Friends with Benefits wanted to hook up that day, so he invented the telephone to facilitate booty calls. Peter Parker didn't have the proportional strength of a spider, so he got himself bitten by a radioactive one and enabled precisely that.

The point is that, in science, it's at least as important to look at the things which don't exist as it is to utilize the things which do; thusly, we have speculative science. Things that were unthinkable a few hundred years ago—flight, long-distance communication, and living past the age of forty—are now commonplace. Someday you may travel to work simply by beaming there, Maybe you'll undo accounting errors by traveling back in time and fixing them before they even happened, or perhaps you'll decide that there just aren't enough yous out there.

Cloning: What to Do When You Meet You

Using science to create copies of yourself isn't as far off as you might think. Scientists have already cloned sheep, mice, and puppies, and who doesn't want more puppies? Someday you'll probably be able to get a duplicate of yourself for safe keeping, but then the question becomes *what do you with you?* You'd be surprised by the number of options that open up when you've got a second you around. You can get twice as much accomplished, you have someone else around backing you up in every argument, and you'll never be lonely since you'll always be there to keep you company. There's also a variety of fun, wholesome activities which will be doubly fun with another player who will always offer an equal challenge to you, not to mention plenty of not-so-wholesome activities that you've thought about doing but are ashamed to admit to.[2]

Once you start cloning yourself, you'll need to be careful that your clones don't start making clones of themselves. Like a copying machine, each successive duplication will be of lower quality, until eventually your clones will come out hunch-backed, buck-toothed, and *Firefly*-hating.[3] Even if they don't create a deformed army, they'll lead

---

[2] Yes, if you clone yourself and then have sex with said clone, it's gay. It's also tremendously narcissistic.

[3] Or maybe they'll start getting superpowers. For more information on superpowered clones, check out the animated webseries *House of Cosbys*, about a Bill Cosby superfan who cloned himself an army of Cosby clones, each with their own specializations. For example, Bathtub Cosby is always in the bathtub. Curiosity Cosby is unquenchably Curious. Cosby Team Tri-Osby is a trio of super-powered, evil-fighting Cosbys.

to problems in other ways. In Michael Keaton's gripping documentary, *Multiplicity*, the Keaton-ator stars as Doug Kinney, a loving family man who doesn't have enough hours in the day to do all the things that need doing. After a little helpful super-science enters the picture, however, suddenly there's a whole pile of Dougs running around doing things and having conversations that Doug Prime doesn't remember, but ends up taking the heat for. Calvin of *Calvin and Hobbes* fame experiences the same thing when he used his duplication machine to create copies of himself to go to school in his stead. As expected, his duplicates didn't want to go to school any more than he did. The moral of these stories? Think twice before cloning yourself for personal gain.

Ten Things Most People Would Use Their Clones For

10 | Doing their chores for them.

9 | Training against them in a sport of choice, like tennis, mathletics, or Quidditch.

8 | Backup organs.

7 | Testing out new haircuts to see whether they look stupid or not.

6 | Practical jokes.

5 | Impractical jokes.

4 | Forcing them to fight in a gladiatorial arena for their own depraved amusement.

3 | Staying home from work while simultaneously going to work and earning a paycheck.

2 | Kissing practice.

1 | Target practice.

Meta-Humans: Surviving in a World of Cardboard

If you want to be a superhero, odds are you're going to want superpowers.[4] Modern science may not be able to grant us ice breath or X-ray vision, but the size, strength, and intelligence of today's humans seem superhuman when compared to the primitive little dummies running around a thousand years ago. Much of that has to do with the increased quality of life we enjoy, but, as we progress, genetic engineering will probably play a key factor in the advancement of humanity. Currently we can grow backup body parts on rats, give mice glow-in-the-dark bones, and breed dogs who can sneeze all their fur off on command.[5] While you're not going to find any phosphorescent people wandering the streets any time soon, scientists have become increasingly adept at tinkering with our chromosomal makeup. Who knows, soon you may be able to order superpowers as easily as looking through a comic book and telling the doctor which hero you'd want to copy.

Ten Superheroes Whose Powers People Would Copy If They Could

10 | KITTY PRYDE
Power: intangibility

9 | JEAN GREY
Powers: telekinesis/telepathy

8 | THE FLASH
Power: super speed

7 | THE INVISIBLE WOMAN
Powers: projecting forcefields, and if I have to tell you what else the Invisible Woman can do you need to pay closer attention

6 | HYDROMAN/THE HUMAN TORCH/SANDMAN/MAGNETO/GRAVITY ...
or any other character who can manipulate one of the basic elements or forces of the universe

---

[4] Unless you're Batman, in which case, sorry about your parents, dude.
[5] Don't be too impressed; they can really only do this trick once every couple of months.

If you're interested in more stories about genetic modification, check out the following books, movies, TV shows, and video games: *Animorphs, Orphan Black, Resident Evil,*[6] *Dark Angel,* The *Moreau* series*, 2312, Bioshock, Exosquad, Gattaca,* and the *Metal Gear Solid* series.

While we can currently modify the gene pool in some truly impressive ways, it may be a while before we discover a tonic that grants the user the ability to throw lightning, or the right level of radiation to make a spider-bite give you powers rather than a tumor. There is, however, one type of human enhancement which is already here: cybernetics.

Go-Go Gadgets!

As of this writing, there are machines to regulate the flow of blood to and from the heart, implants to grant hearing to formerly deaf individuals, and cybernetic limbs to

5 | **DOCTOR STRANGE**
Powers: magic, dude!

4 | **STORM**
Power: weather manipulation

3 | **MR. FANTASTIC**[7]
Powers: elasticity; shapeshifting; near invulnerability
to bludgeoning, force, and piercing attacks

2 | **WOLVERINE**
Powers: rapid regeneration, enhanced senses, being awesome

1 | **SUPERMAN**
Powers: super speed, super strength, super endurance, flight, heat vision, x-ray vision,
invulnerability, enhanced senses

[6] The video game series, not the movies. The games are generally good, but your mileage may vary on the film series.
[7] Most women's reaction: the ability to stretch my body into any shape? "It's pretty useful, I guess, but it seems like it should be lower on the list." Most men's reaction? "The ability to stretch any part of my body into any shape or size? Why isn't this #1?"

Steve Austin easily lifts a car.

Steve Austin lifts a tree as though it were a twig.

Steve Austin stops a runaway train.

replace missing meaty limbs. While most people are more man than machine,[8] [9] that ratio may not always stay the same, and that'll probably be a good thing. These mechanical enhancements are one of the many ways humanity can use its intelligence to defeat the physical limitations bestowed upon us by evolution.

The Six Million Dollar Man is one of the earliest bits of pop culture to bring public awareness to the concept of bionics. Sure, the weekly struggles of bionic man Steve Austin (and his extended bionic family) may not have been the most realistic depiction of cybernetics, but it let the general public know that it existed, and helped excite future scientists into researching the field once they became adults. It also lead to that slow motion/*wa-na-na-na-na* special effects combo that has become synonymous with low budget superpower use.[10]

If Steve Austin and Agent Maxwell Smart had a baby, that baby would have been *Inspector Gadget.* Voiced by Agent Smart himself, Don Adams, Inspector Gadget fought Dr. Claw and the forces of evil using his variety of implanted bionic gizmos, like his signature rollerskate feet, helicopter hat, and telephone thumb/pinky. While the good Inspector's gadgets got most of the attention in the fight against evil, it was his niece, Penny, doing the real work. She and her loyal dog, Brain, were always behind the scenes, helping the good-natured, but dim-witted, Inspector solve crimes and stay alive.

For more bionically enhanced shows, check out: *The Bionic Woman, Bionic Six,*

---

[8] Except for Gary Busey. There's no way that dude isn't secretly a robot who short-circuited and flipped his shit. Just look at him! He's so twitchy and crazy!

[9] Oh, and Ronald McDonald. Legend has it he's more hamburger than man.

[10] Did anybody else find it weird that *The Six Million Dollar Man* would depict Steve Austin's super speed by showing him in slow motion? Seems counter-intuitive if you ask me.

Robocop: The TV Series, Max Steel, Gadget Boy & Heather/Gadget Boy's Adventures in History, and the hilariously lame *Jake 2.0.*

Of course, not every scientist is content with merely combining man and machine. Some want to make men out of machines—I'm talking androids, people. It may be a while before you see any humanoid robots riding the subway next to you, but don't be surprised in twenty years when GoogleBots start transforming and rolling out all around the country.

Data

"I am ... fully functional."

It ain't easy being an android. Humans make jokes you don't get, or react in unexpected ways, or make inexplicable googly eyes at each other from across the room. *Star Trek: The Next Generation's* Data made the best of being stuck in a ship full of meatbags, though, and over the course of the series he grew from a cold-hearted machine into basically an albino dude who never had to call in sick. While Data could have easily been a duller-than-rocks character, Brent Spiner's sharp sense of humor shone through in his performance, bringing out the funny at unexpected moments. Oddly enough, level-headed Data scored big with *TNG*'s female fans. Spiner reasoned that Data had an "accessible personality," and his tryst with Tasha Yar makes the two of them the first characters to get laid on that particular Enterprise (NCC-1701-D).

If you're nuts about androids, check out the following shows, movies, video games, and books: *Star Trek: The Next Generation, Big O, The Hitchhiker's Guide to the Galaxy, Red Dwarf, Not Quite Human,* and the *Persona* series.

Time Travel: How Not to Accidentally Become Your Own Mother

Fact: 83 percent of all physicists got into the field in the hopes of inventing the first time machine. Who can blame them? Human beings are the smartest things around—we've made pretty much everything in the known universe into our butt-monkeys, but one of the few things we've yet to master is *time*. Time marches inexorably forward—no matter how much we wrap ourselves around its ankles and scream for it to slow down. But just because we've yet to bend the streams of time into something a little more usable doesn't mean we'll ever stop trying.

History's Five Most Notable Attempts At Time Travel

Where: Moscow, Russia
Who: Doctor Ivan Ivonoff Ivankovich
When: 1911
What: During a test of the idiom about cats landing on their feet, Ivankovich tied two felines back-to-back and dropped them from a height of half a meter. Since cats always land on their feet, and since it was physically impossible for *both* cats to land on their feet, he reasoned that they would instead spin infinitely in place above the ground, both landing and not landing on their feet, creating a tear in time and space. Instead what he got was a gaggle of very pissed off cats.

Where: Sedona, Arizona
Who: Arthur Rigberry and The Psycho-Delic Sound
When: 1963
What: Rigberry, lead singer/guitarist for the Psycho-Delic Sound, consumed what he believed to be over a pound of brownies laced with a hallucinogenic substance (but were actually regular brownies). He then informed his band mates that, if they could find the right combination of sounds, they'd master time and space. The band played for nearly seven hours until drummer Steven "Scads" Fisher threw up from the stress, and bassist Gregory "Smoofer" Smooferman smashed his instrument over Rigberry's head for insisting they play "Stairway to Heaven" for the nineteenth consecutive time.

Several theories posit how time travel might be possible. One theory roughly states that, should we find a way of traveling faster than the speed of light, we'll crack the temporal barrier and move through time at an anomalous rate. Another theory involves the use of wormholes to act as the quantum physics equivalent to the warp pipes found in *Super Mario Bros.*

Scientists have held several events and conventions in the hopes of enticing any time travelers to visit them, such as MIT's Time Traveler Convention, but thus far, none have bitten. Is it because no time traveler was interested in visiting the events? Does time travel involve the use of parallel timelines, thusly making it impossible to visit the convention occurring in our

3

Where: Brazilia, Brazil
Who: Estafani Santos
When: 1985

What: Santos, an expert surfer, attempted to surf faster than the speed of light. Most experts agree the only thing she managed to surf that day was a truly gnarly set of waves.

Where: Boise, Idaho
Who: Randy and Andi Weaver
When: 2009

What: Suburban couple Randy and Andi Weaver sat down to watch *The Notebook.* When the movie ended, the Weavers claimed to have no recollection of watching it, and surmised that they'd time traveled. Later tests indicated that they fell asleep.

Where: Oakview, California
Who: Unknown
When: 2005

What: A man placed a wanted ad in the paper requesting for someone to go back in time with him. "This is not a joke," the ad states. "You'll get paid after we get back. Must bring your own weapons. Safety not guaranteed. I have only done this once before." It's unknown whether anyone responded to his ad, nor if they were successful in their mission.

"prime" timeline? Or, in keeping with assumptions of not violating causality, time travelers can either only travel forward, or only travel back to the point when the first time machine was invented. Regardless, most physics hopefuls believe that time travel will occur, eventually, and will keep trying to be the first to break that chronological barrier, no matter the cost.

Virtual Reality: I Know Kung Fu

In the Wachowskis' classic romantic comedy *The Matrix,* machines have overtaken the human race and enslaved them to act as bio-batteries for their evil, machine-y ways. To keep humanity docile, the machines created a computerized virtual reality matrix to act as a surrogate for these individuals' real lives. While this plotline served as the center for some truly awesome action sequences (and some wonky philosophical idealogy from the Wachowskis) it also raised another interesting point: What if the entirety of human existence is actually being generated by a hyper-advanced computer system?

That begets larger theoretical concerns, like whether other people in such a system are real or if they're just virtual philosophical zombies, i.e. beings that behave as if they're real people but lack the internal thoughts and motivations of a real person. Scientists have thought of numerous ways to prove whether or not we're trapped in some computerized system, but, as science finds time and time again, it's difficult to absolutely disprove something. Also, should computer technology advance to that level we may be able to utilize it for our own trans-humanistic needs, perhaps even achieving an immortality, of sorts, by uploading ourselves into a computer system and living on through it. It's not an ideal immortality, of course, but it's better than nothing.

 Totally Dope Ways of Becoming Immortal

- Uploading yourself to a computer system and becoming living data.
- Getting bitten by a vampire. And I'm talking about the cool kind of vampire, not... sparklies.

- Being a Highlander-style immortal and permanently camping out on holy ground.
- Finding a genie and wishing for immortality.[11] Specify that you're wishing for eternal youth, otherwise that jerk might make you live forever, but as a really old person. Make sure to wish for some invulnerability while you're at it—no sense in not aging if catching a cold or getting stung by a million bees will do you in.
- Make a dark pact involving the sacrifice of innocent lives/souls.[12]
- Find some super-science way of achieving immortality, perhaps by becoming a cyborg, or by creating a potion that stops the aging process.
- Cloning younger versions of yourself and then transferring your consciousness into their bodies.[13]

Ghostbusting Makes Me Feel Good

What happens when we die? Some speculate there's a judgment-based afterlife awaiting us, with our ultimate destination being dependent on whether we were pretty cool people or evil douchebags. Others believe that we're reincarnated and born again as entirely new beings—rebooting our franchises. Still others suspect that we don't move on, we convert into ethereal versions of ourselves and float around haunting graveyards, Ouija Boards, and the cookie jar.[14]

If you're watching a television show about ghosts, odds are it's a reality show built around variations of getting a jerk camera crew to follow a bunch of jerks around in the dark until some other jerk throws a shoe or something and everyone pretends to get scared. It's not all junk, though, not as long as we've got *Being Human,* a show about a vampire, a werewolf, and a ghost struggling to deal with twenty-something melodrama while also dealing with being creatures of the night. *Being Human*'s resident ghost, Sally Malik, has had to contend with all sorts of ghoulish conundrums, such as ghost-on-ghost combat, reapers, and witches trying to do witchy, evil things to them.

Most ghostly books are short story collections, like Roald Dahl's *Book of Ghost Stories,* and *Scary Stories to Tell in the Dark,* the latter of which has some of the most

---

[11] PRO TIP: Should you ever find a wish-granting genie, wish for more wishes. If that genie can't grant additional wishes beyond the standard three, wish for more genies.

[12] PRO TIP: Don't do this. Don't be that guy. Nobody likes that guy.

[13] PRO TIP: This, too, is kind of an a-hole move.

[14] Everyone knows that the cookie jar is haunted—it's what my mom told me when I'd try to get cookies. Didn't yours?

unbelievably chilling art you'll ever see.[15] Video games may be the medium that makes the most liberal use of ghosties, even spanning multiple genres. *Fatal Frame* gives a twist on traditional horror gaming by forcing players to avoid lots of killer ghosts and take lots of pictures of killer ghosts like an unholy version of Instagram. *Ghost Trick: Phantom Detective* charges the player with the task of solving his/her own murder and requires the completion of numerous brain-tingling puzzles. *The Luigi's Mansion* adventure games star Mario's green-clad brother Luigi doing what he, apparently, does best: busting ghosts.

The Ghostbusters

"I love this plan! I'm excited to be a part of it!"
-Dr. Peter Venkman, PhD in psychology (and parapsychology[16])

While the boys in brown may not always be the best scientists, when ghosts come a-knocking, who you gonna call? They're also a great example of how a team should work, geeky or otherwise, managing to combine together to accomplish far greater things than they could individually. Winston is the team's muscle—this hard-working everyman has unparalleled skills when it comes to the rough-and-tumble part of ghostbusting. Ray's the heart, full of child-like innocence and enthusiasm for every weird and wondrous thing that comes their way. Egon is, obviously, the brain (though he'd tell you that the ladies are less interested in his brain and more in his epididymis). Peter? He's the mouth, the voice-box for the group. His moral core's a little shakier, but beneath his snarky exterior lays a heart of (probably fake) gold.

---

[15] Later printings changed the pictures to far less imaginative (and less gruesome) artwork. I guess the printers reasoned that the original art was too scary for kids. Booooo! If I endured a constant stream of nightmares as a kid, so can today's children!

[16] I've always wondered where in the hell Peter got his PhD in Parapsychology. Who even offers that as a graduate program?

 ## Tips for Wannabe Ghost Hunters

- Travel in groups of three. Groups of two or fewer generally get slaughtered. Groups of three or more (who stick *together)* rarely run into trouble.

- Be prepared for all kinds of ghosts: powerful ghosts, friendly ghosts, racist ghosts, ghosts with the most, etc.

- At any time, think to yourself: Is this something someone would be doing before the opening credits of a horror movie or an episode of *Supernatural?* If the answer is yes, quit doing that, and start doing something smarter.

- If you see a ghost dog, pet it only so long as it seems friendly. If you see a copy of *Ghost Dog: Way of the Samurai,* watch it only if no kids are around.

- Don't be a priest of any kind, and *especially* not a lapsed priest struggling with your faith. Those dudes place at the top of pretty much every ghost's hit list.

- If you encounter a haunted house, bust out every window and smash off every door before going in. It's hard for a ghost to lock you in the house if there's nothing to lock.

- Ghosts respond well to the scent of citrus. Do with that what you will.

- If a ghost invites you to its wedding, it's unlikely they actually want you to attend. Generally they only invite the living to be polite.

- Bring plenty of anti-ghost supplies: salt, cast iron weapons, magic charms, cameras, proton packs, etc.

- If you're checking out a haunted location, do it early in the *day,* ya idjit.

- Bone up on your local history. This way you're prepared for the ghost's powers and its rules, plus it'll feel flattered that you know about it.

- Try talking to the ghost about things *they* like— their past, what it's like being a ghost, whether or not they want to split a meatball sub with you, etc.

- Try not to be the first, or the last, person to enter or exit a room.
- If you hear the ghostly sounds of children laughing, *get the hell out of there.*

Cryptozoology: Fancy Talk For 'Lookin' Fer Bigfoot'

Science has done a pretty thorough job of documenting everything there is to document on Earth,[17] but that doesn't discourage plenty of enthusiastic explorers for hunting for *That Which They Think Exists, But Don't Really Have Proof Of Except That One Time They Kind Of Saw It Out Of The Corner Of Their Eye While Taking A Whiz Against A Tree.* I speak, of course, of cryptids—creatures whose existences seem plausible, but haven't been proven.

Ten of the Most Sought-After/Hottest Cryptids

10 | BIGFOOT
Habitat: Forest/mountains
Special qualities/abilities: Human-like intelligence; lustrous coat of fur
Hottness: 8/10 - Too Hott 2 Touch

9 | THE LOCH NESS MONSTER
Habitat: The Loch Ness
Special qualities/abilities: Water breathing; photosynthesis
Hottness: 7/10 - One Spicy Meatball

8 | EL CHUPACABRA
Habitat: Mexico
Special qualities/abilities: Mariachi skills
Hottness: 6/10 - One Toasty Tortilla

7 | THE JERSEY DEVIL
Habitat: The Pine Barrens of Southern New Jersey
Special qualities/abilities: Steroid use; orange tan
Hottness: 4/10 - Not Bad. Okay, Kind of Bad

"The greatest monster since 'KING KONG'" —THE POST

"The most realistic horrifying film ever!"

BIGFOOT

breeds with anything...

COLOR

---

[17] Except for the really, really deep parts of the ocean. Crap is crazy down there.

6 | THE LONG ISLAND LICKING MAN

Habitat: Long Island, New York City
Special qualities/abilities: Licking
Hottness: 2/10 - Would Not Bang

5 | MANBEARPIG

Habitat: Where the weather suits his clothes
Special qualities/abilities: Fire-breathing; invisibility; mathematics
Hottness: 3/10 - Would Not Pork

4 | THE MOTHMAN

Habitat: Point Pleasant, West Virginia; anywhere with porch lights
Special qualities/abilities: Precognition
Hottness: 5/10 - Lukewarm

3 | DOVER DEMON

Habitat: Dover, Massachusetts
Special qualities/abilities: Telepathy
Hottness: 5/10 - Lukewarm

2 | SLENDERMAN

Habitat: Playgrounds; the forest
Special qualities/abilities: Teleportation; silent movement; Darkness (Sorcerer/Wizard 2) as a free action each round; child-stealing; immortality; imperviousness to all known weapons; fancies a nice suit
Hottness: 10/10 - OMG Wut A Babe

1 | CARL LUNKMAN

Habitat: His mother's basement
Special qualities/abilities: Can eat twenty pounds of nachos in twenty minutes. World-record holder for most audible farts ever recorded inside a porta potty. Once wrote a two-hundred-page document detailing the system of "Poetry Combat" that is the conflict device in his eleven-hundred-page unfinished novel, *The Devin Darkness and Th'randuriel Th'Th'Lgaren'Th Chronicles Book I: Vengeancedetta*.
Hottness: 1/10 - Do Not Want.

THE RANSOME EXPEDITION TO LOCH NESS

DAVID W. PORTER

The Five Types of Aliens Most Commonly Found on Earth

None of the tips on pages 29 and 30 are necessary if you're the sort who believes that there are aliens living among us, disguised as humans. Why they'd move to Earth, of all places, is beyond me, but hey, it could happen. There've been a number of reported alien species living on Earth, but a few stand out above the rest

5 | ROSWELL GREYS

Appearance: Large, grey beings with dark, oval shaped eyes.

Alien abilities: Telepathy and unfathomably advanced technology.

Known for: Abducting people and probing pretty much any hole they can cram something into.

4 | REPTILIANS

Appearance: Reptilian humanoids who disguise themselves as humans in order to infiltrate our society.

Alien abilities: High levels of intelligence, Machiavellian skills of manipulation.

Known for: Trying to rule Earth from within. They're also quite fond of drinking blood and eating human flesh, which isn't cool.

3 | KRYPTIONIANS

Appearance: Humanoids who look like us, but are more awesome.

Alien abilities: A variety of powers derived from our yellow sun's energy, including (but not limited to): super speed, super strength, invulnerability, heat vision, ice breath, X-ray vision, and flight.

Known for: Wearing suits with the letter S on them, pretending to be clumsy.

2 | DONKLES

Appearance: Small, fuzzy creatures often disguised as tumbleweeds.

Alien abilities: Sloth-like pacifism and laziness. They gain energy via photosynthesis.

Known for: A Donkle will often reveal itself in the presence of a hat. Hats are quite fashionable on the Donkle homeworld of DonkDonkDonklia[18] and many Donkles come to Earth as a means of obtaining our exotic Earth hats. They're also big fans of *Team Fortress 2.*

1 | KLARVIANS

Appearance: Squat, orange beings with long faces, no eyes, and unusually flat tongues.

Alien abilities: An extraordinary sense of taste.

Known for: Being obsessed with butter, lard, and fried foods. Many believe Paula Deen to be the leader of the Klarvians, but, to the best of our knowledge, she's just a chick who loves two things: country-fried cooking and old-timey racism. Those idiot Klarvians revere her as some sort of messiah.

---

[18] Found in the Donk nebula.

Monsters in My Pocket, and Aliens in My Underwear

Aliens have been a pop culture staple for years. The early twentieth century gave us plenty of serial films and comic books about little green men, but it wasn't until the UFO movies of the 1950s that we saw a dramatic boom in the popularity of aliens in popular culture.[19] The universe is a big, big place, so it makes sense to think that there should be other intelligent life out there. The fine folks over at SETI[20] spend their days using diligent, empirical methods to broadcast our existence into space in the hopes that some nice aliens out there might stumble across it and come knocking on our door with smiles on their faces and pies in hand. But just because the folks at SETI are specialized masters in the field of astronomy, communication, and spacestuffology, doesn't mean that enthusiastic laygeeks such as us can't get in on the UFO spotting, too.

 ## How to Meet Martians and Influence Aliens

- Stargazing is a cheap, easy way to keep an eye out for landing/crash-landing aliens, although realize that stargazers are usually the first to go in any alien invasion movie. If you're going to go check out a potential alien crash site, stream it online so that (1) if you meet an alien, there's proof for others to see, and (2) if said alien kills you, we'll know to cancel your credit cards before it can use them.

- If you do meet an alien, *keep still.* When animals encounter something they don't understand, they tend to wig out and start running around like total spazzoids. If you want to make friends with these otherworldly visitors, you'll need to prove that you're smarter than the average bear, and the easiest way to do that is to react calmly to their presence.

- For crying out loud, don't bring a gun with you. If these beings have mastered interstellar technology, it's unlikely that something as simple as a *gun* would do any good against them. If they're hostile, bringing a gun will make them kill you that much faster and with that much more smugness. If they're friendly, it just makes you look like a dick.

- Observe what they do, and adjust your own behavior accordingly. If the

---

[19] Coincidentally, we saw a spike in the frequency of UFO sightings at right around the same time. Hmm. How odd.
[20] The Search for Extra-Terrestrial Intelligence.

aliens sniff each other's butts as greetings, be prepared to embrace their culture and get a whiff of some cheeks.

- If you're expecting interplanetary guests, put out a bowl of snacks. Chex Mix works for nearly any occasion.
- Becoming an astronaut seems like a good way to meet aliens, although it's a bit more of a timesink than simply buying a telescope and watching the stars at night.
- Put an ad on *Craigslist* stating that you're looking to meet some local aliens.

Inventors, Visionaries, and Other Geeks You Should Be Thanking

Of course, where would speculative science be without *real* science? As you're well aware, we geeks are the movers and the shakers of history—without geeks to think our way up to the next echelon of human evolution, our species would probably still be wearing animal skins and sitting in caves chucking dookie at each other. Though there are many fields for knowledge-hungry geeks to choose from, one thing that unites all geeks is our passion for excelling in our fields. The greats all have that same burning desire to learn more, to become better, and to improve the condition of his or her fellow man. Let's take a walk back through some of history's greatest geeks, because without them we'd still be cave-dwelling dook-chuckers.

ARCHIMEDES (287 BC – 212 BC)

Field: Mathematics, astronomy, physics

Most Known For: Archimedes' principle, Archimedes' Screw, the fulcrum, and a death ray.

Most People Don't Know That: Archimedes had a dog named Barkimedes.

NIKOLA TESLA (July 10, 1856 – Jan. 7, 1943)

Field: Electrical engineering, physics, and futurism

Most Known For: Alternating current, early X-ray technology, the Tesla coil. Also possibly death rays, teleportation devices, cloning machines, and mechanical crickets.

Most People Don't Know That: He and fellow electrician/inventor Thomas Edison had quite the rivalry going. Edison was the clear antagonist in the relationship, often going out of his way to taunt or discredit Tesla.[21]

ROBERT LISTON (Oct. 28, 1794 – Dec. 7, 1847)

Field: Nineteenth-century surgery

Most Known For: Unbelievable surgical/amputation speed, which, during this era of crude medical practices, was one of the few reliable ways to increase the likelihood of patient survival.

Most People Don't Know That: Liston approached surgery the way Wolverine might approach surgery—like a berserker beast. Once, while amputating a man's leg, Liston also, in his zeal, accidentally removed the patient's testicles. During another surgery, he amputated the patient's leg in 2 1/2 minutes, but the patient died of gangrene in the hospital. During that same surgery, Liston also accidentally sliced off two of his assistant's fingers, and that assistant also died of gangrene in the hospital. *And,* in his enthusiasm, Liston accidentally slashed the overcoat of an onlooker, who suffered a heart attack from the fright and died. This is the only known operation in history to have a 300% mortality rate.[22]

JOHANN GUTENBERG (1395 – Feb. 3, 1468)

Field: Publishing

Most Known For: The invention of movable type printing.

Most People Don't Know That: Gutenberg was nutso about shoes. Dude owned over twenty pairs of shoes, which would be like a modern person owning roughly a billion.

---

[21] Some of these "Most People Don't Know Thats" are jokes, but this one is actually true. Edison may have been a genius, but he was a real jerk to Tesla.

[22] This stuff about Robert Liston may sound insane, but it's also true.

GEORGE WASHINGTON CARVER
(Jan. 1864 – Jan. 5, 1943)

Field: Botany

Most Known For: Facilitating countless improvements to the way farms are handled, the technology used to grow crops, and for finding an insane number of uses for the peanut.

Most People Don't Know That: GWC declared Reese's Peanut Butter Cups to be an "inglorious misuse of the noblest of legumes."

LEONARDO DA VINCI (April 15, 1452 – May 2, 1519)

Field: Freaking everything

Most Known For: Mona Lisa, The Last Supper, countless inventions and ideas.

Most People Don't Know That: Technically, da Vinci never died. He invented a time machine and used it to teleport right behind you.

GREGOR MENDEL (July 20, 1822 – Jan. 6, 1884)

Field: Genetics

Most Known For: Fathering the field of genetics.

Most People Don't Know That: Mendel's beat-boxing skills were unparalleled.

BARBARA MCCLINTOCK (June 16, 1902 – Sept. 2, 1992)

Field: Botany and cytogenics

Most Known For: Mapping the genetic structure of corn

Most People Don't Know That: McClintock may have conducted much of her research on corn, but she refused to eat it, calling it "way too yellow."

EDWARD OSBORNE "E.O." WILSON (June 10, 1929 –)

Field: Entomology, biology, and sociobiology

Most Known For: Fathering the field of sociobiology and studying a crapload of ants.

Most People Don't Know That: E.O. loved the feel of a good pair of socks.

CAROLINE HERSCHEL (March 16, 1750 – Jan. 9, 1848)

Field: Astronomy

Most Known For: Increasing the number of known star clusters from one-hundred to twenty-five hundred.

Most People Don't Know That: In addition to being the first woman to discover a comet, she was also the first person to come up with that "put black varnish on the eyepiece of a telescope so that when people look through it, they end up with a black ring around the eye" prank.

CHARLES DARWIN (Feb. 12, 1809 – April 19, 1882)

Field: Naturalism

Most Known For: The Theory of Evolution.

Most People Don't Know That: Darwin never got a chance to play *Pokemon*, but if he had, he undoubtedly would have approved.

CARL LINNAEUS (May 23, 1707 – Jan. 10, 1778)

Field: Botany, biology, and zoology

Most Known For: Creating modern taxonomy.

Most People Don't Know That: Linnaeus refused to classify any species of llama, calling them "nature's greatest bastard."

LISE MEITNER (Nov. 7, 1878 – Oct. 27, 1968)

Field: Physics

Most Known For: Discovering nuclear fission.

Most People Don't Know That: After discovering nuclear fission, Lise would always exit a room by telling people that she "had to split."

GALILEO (Feb. 15, 1564 – Jan. 8, 1642)

Field: Astronomy, physics, and mathematics

Most Known For: Heliocentrism and telescopic observation.

Most People Don't Know That: Before coming up with the theory of heliocentrism, which states that the sun is the center of our galaxy, Galileo came up with the theory of Italianatidaeocentrism, theorizing that the Earth revolved around a small duck outside of Pisa, Italy.

MARIE CURIE (Nov. 7, 1867 – July 4, 1934)

Field: Physics and chemistry

Most Known For: Her research into radioactivity.

Most People Don't Know That: Marie Curie wrote volumes of fan fiction about Baron Munchausen.

SIGMUND FREUD (May 6, 1856 – Sept. 23, 1939)

Field: Psychology

Most Known For: Psychoanalysis.

Most People Don't Know That: Freud believed that cocaine was a super drug, and extolled the virtues of the substance at length.[23]

---

[23] True as well. Freud was a major cokehead.

WILHELM WUNDT (Aug. 16, 1832 – Aug. 31, 1920)

Field: Social psychology

Most Known For: Establishing the sub-field of social psychology as a distinct science; founding the first true psychology laboratory.

Most People Don't Know That: Wundt would often absentmindedly doodle ladybugs on his notebooks.

ALBERT EINSTEIN (March 14, 1879 – April 18, 1955)

Field: Physics

Most Known For: The theory of relativity and a number of other physics theories, theorems, hypotheses, and hypopotamuses.

Most People Don't Know That: Einstein really liked the sound of his name being said backwards, and would occasionally ask people to introduce him as Nietsnie Trebla.

BENJAMIN FRANKLIN (Jan. 17, 1706 – April 17, 1790)

Field: Physics, literature, music ... you name it, and Ben was probably into it.

Most Known For: Helping found America, inventing the bifocals and lightning rod, and proving that lightning was electricity, *not,* as so many erroneously claim, that he discovered electricity.

Most People Don't Know That: Ben Franklin was a nudist.[24]

---

[24] Evidence suggests that this, too, is true. You're welcome for the image of Ben Franklin's flabby physique in the buff.

Chapter 2

Six Seasons and a Movie:
Why We Love Television

Watching a movie or television show can feel similar to being in a relationship. Movies are the more independent, aloof paramours—they may or may not decide to open up to you, and whether they do or don't, it's just how they are, and you gotta deal with it. They're intense, they're brief, but hopefully they're memorable. Your relationship with television shows, however, provides an ongoing experience. Sometimes the magic fades in your relationship; maybe the show's not as lively as it used to be, or maybe you're not the same person you were when you first started watching. But, if you're lucky, the show will grow and mature with you. When you need a laugh, it's there with a quick joke. If you're ready for a good cry, it'll kill off your favorite character with a death both befitting and heroic. And if you're thinking of dumping the show in favor of something better, well, sometimes it'll jump the shark[25] at the right moment, letting you know that splitting up is the right thing to do.

---

[25] Jump the shark: that point when a show, which had been steadily declining in quality, becomes irrevocably bad, and is usually demarcated by a gimmicky, outlandish scheme to garner ratings. The name of this trope stems from the episode of *Happy Days* in which the Fonz, in his leather jacket and a pair of swimming trunks, jumped over a shark during a surfing contest. Any fans the show still had left felt a piece of themselves die that day over the sheer banal stupidity of this episode.

Good or bad, television shows provide reliable entertainment, which is part of why we love them. Television's longer format also allows for more in-depth storytelling. Like a good book, a TV series can dive deep into its characters and world, really exploring everything that's unique and interesting about it.

Oddly enough, though, modern television fans may not actually watch *television*. Perhaps you caught up on *Lost* via your laptop, maybe *The Walking Dead* stumbles its way onto your iPad every week, or maybe you enjoy acting out *Breaking Bad* as a weekly, drug-addled puppet show, but the point is that the method of delivery doesn't matter—it's the heart of television we adore. It's a medium filled with weekly doses of stories that amaze us, worlds that intrigue us, and characters we love, hate, and love to hate.[26]

Five of the Most Heart-Breaking Episodes in Sci-Fi/Fantasy Television[27]

5 | **"The End of Time (Part Two)"** – *Doctor Who*
The reason it's sad: The tenth doctor doesn't want to go.

4 | **"The Real Folk Blues (Part Two)"** – *Cowboy Bebop*
The reason it's sad: "Bang."

3 | **"The Candidate"** – *Lost*
The reason it's sad: The submarine sinks.

2 | **"Jurassic Bark"** – *Futurama*
The reason it's sad: Seymour waits.

1 | **"The Body"** – *Buffy the Vampire Slayer*
The reason it's sad: It's the most brutally realistic depiction of loss and grief ever put to screen.

---

[26] In this book, I'm going to make fun of a lot of TV shows. And movies. And lots of other things. Just because I make fun of them doesn't mean you should feel even a little bit bad about liking them, because 1. You should never feel bad about the stuff you think is cool, and 2. Just because you mock something doesn't mean you dislike it. Hell, I make fun of *Dragon Ball Z* all the time, but I also eat up every single episode like a hungry dog being loosed from his pen.

[27] Honorable mention to the *Torchwood*'s entire "Children of Earth" miniseries.

FANTASY SHOWS:
WHAT'S YOUR FANTASY?

Fantasy and science fiction share a lot of common elements, with their ability to use unreal situations to provide perspective on very *real* situations, but one thing fantasy shows have going for them that sci-fi shows don't? *They don't have to explain jack crap.* Want to have someone turned into a mermaid for an episode? Do it. On a sci-fi show, you'd have to come up with some kind of DNA manipulation, or body transference machine, *something.* Fantasy can handwave those kinds of things away with a name and a curse. "It's Bigby's Mermaid Malady," the show's resident magic expert explains, "and the only cure is *more cowbell.*"

Buffy the Vampire Slayer took advantage of that unreality, and, at the same time, somehow managed to ground the fantasy with some real-feeling characters. Buffy, Xander, Willow, Giles, and the rest of the Scoobies spent a lot of time hitting the books with a vengeance (mostly) off-camera. When battling the forces of evil on a daily basis, one simply *must* do the appropriate research to go along with it. In addition to being pro-books, *Buffy* was about as pro-feminist and pro-good-storytelling as you can get. Joss Whedon, known to a portion of the public as "The *Avengers* Guy," created a show with one of feminism's most enduring heroes, Buffy Summers, as well as a cast of geeks and misfits who helped the real-life geeks and misfits watching them every week feel at home—yours truly included.

At the beginning of the series, snark-tastic Xander and bookwormy Willow are the kind of nerdy characters most high school shows would have relegated to the periphery. When ex-cheerleader Buffy arrives on the scene, the "in-crowd" immediately accepts her, but she finds that she empathizes more with the so-called outcasts than with any of the cool kids. From there, the trio bonds, and each of them discover who they are, as well as what differing brands of greatness they have to offer the world. The main morals of the show end up being two-fold: women empowering women, and that the bonds of friendship and family extend beyond the folks with whom you have a few chromosomes in common.

Willow

"It's just, in high school, knowledge was pretty much frowned upon. You really had to work to learn anything. But here [in college], the energy, the collective intelligence, it's like this force, this penetrating force."

Few characters endure so large of a character arc as Willow. All of *Buffy*'s main characters grow and change from season one to seven, but Willow has what's possibly the most dramatic transformation. The first we see of Willow is a soft-spoken, stuttering girl, mocked by the more popular kids for her intelligence and lack of fashion acumen. As time goes on, however, she finds confidence in knowing who she is and what she's good at. Late in high school, she begins taking pride in her scholastic accomplishments, and studies witchcraft on the side. Given that *Buffy* basically ignores college partway through the fifth season, it's unclear exactly how far Willow travels in academia (she gets her bachelor's degree, right? We can only assume), but her skills in witchcraft grow so fast and so far that, thanks to a massive personal tragedy, she becomes a big black ball of apocalyptic witchiness. From there, she falls—and falls *hard*—but rebuilds herself back up as a force of good. Many nerdy kids find their post-high school experience to be similar to what Willow went through.[28] Those things that others looked down on you for in high school are things which are respected and needed in college and the real world. Willow ends *Buffy* not as the stuttering, mousey girl she was seven years prior, but as a confident woman, poised and ready to handle whatever life throws her way, no matter how difficult or heart-breaking it may be.

---

[28] Outside of the descent into magic-drugs and trying to destroy the world, that is.

Another fantasy show with a flair for ass-kicking women, *Lost Girl*, takes some of the same themes of female empowerment that *Buffy* was so fond of and wraps them up in more of a grown-up pair of leather pants. Bo the succubus (and titular lost girl) is fiercely determined, passionate to an occasional fault, and sexually liberated. Man or woman, black or white, human or Fae—it's all good. Her human BFF, Kenzie, is no slouch in the being awesome department, either. She has spent much of her life as a drifter and a grifter, and while she'd rather die than get a legit job, she'd also lay down her life for her super-ultra-best-friend-forever, Bo, and vice-versa. The two of them spend much of their time traipsing around town, solving otherworldly crimes and fighting off maladjusted supernatural types. The heart of this show is Bo and Kenzie's bromance[29]—these two gals are friends to the end and have each other's back no matter what. Shows such as *Supernatural* are great, but there are *boatloads* of media devoted to the bond between dudes. It's not often that you have a show about two awesome ladies hanging out and making a difference.

Speaking of bro-tacular friendships, there's a question you, dear reader, need to ask yourself: what time is it?

I'll *tell* you what time it is: *ADVENTURE TIME*! Pendleton Ward's surreal animated opus centers around Jake the dog and Finn the human, two heroic buddies who spend their days adventuring and saving the peaceful peoples of the land of Ooo. Few shows manage to capture the sheer joy of living as much as *Adventure Time*. Nearly every episode opens with Finn and Jake dancing, playing around, or just partying their buff booties off. Save the gritty stuff for Frank Miller— *Adventure Time* makes being a hero look dang fun. But, beneath this post-apocalyptic fantasy world lie stories about young romance, maturity, and conquering loneliness.

Finn and Jake have nigh-supreme confidence, and much of that stems from the two friends knowing that they've always got each other's backs. Some of the peripheral characters, however, have surprisingly complex turmoil, which they often veil with their over-the-top personalities. Sure, Marceline the Vampire Queen may shred on her axe and mess with Finn's head about whether she's chaotic evil or totally neutral good, but she also has a string of broken friendships she can't deal with, and some major vampire-demon daddy issues. And Ice King ... well, that poor bastard's just lonely with a capitol L, something everyone, geek or otherwise, can relate to. *Adventure Time* is far more than a hectically hilarious show about two bros having fantasy adventures; it's also a treatise on growing up.

---

[29] Or would it be Sismance? That sounds weird.

For another kid's show that can also be enjoyed by adults, throw on a martial arts gi and check out *Avatar: The Last Airbender*. In a world filled with citizens who can manipulate the four basic elements, Earth, Fire, Air, and Water, there's a single being gifted with control of all four—the Avatar. The Avatars have a global peace-keeping legacy extending back to the dawn of civilization, and when one falls, another rises up to take his/her place as the bearer of this burden. This generation's chosen one, Aang, loves fun, goofing off, and eating, in that order, and wants nothing to do with such seriousness. Together with his pals, he travels the war-torn world, trying to achieve harmony and accept his responsibility without losing his sense of self.

The quest for self is a major theme of *The Last Airbender*. Aang and his tortured rival, Zuko, both struggle to figure out exactly who they are. Aang's fun-loving nature is at odds with his duty as Avatar. Zuko's burning desire to reclaim his honor by capturing the avatar is at odds with Aang's desire to, you know, *stay alive*. The show's mature writing and fantastic world earned it a devoted fanbase ... and a terrible, *terrible* M. Night Shyamalan movie adaptation.

If you're going to get invested in the *Airbender* series, its follow-up, *The Legend of Korra*, is worth a look as well. The early episodes do flounder a bit between sluggishly moving the story along and blasting through it too quickly, but the show still has a fantastic visual style, interesting setting, and a solid protagonist in the athletic and confident Korra.

Ah, *Community*. On the surface, it seems to be a show about a disparate group of community college students coming together to find a second chance at life. After you watch it for a while, however, it'll become clear that this situation comedy leans closer to a fantasy-comedy than anything else. There've been pillow civil wars, Dungeons and Dragons games, and a Halloween zombie episode featuring *actual zombies*. That's right. It's not a dream, or a spooky story, or some other kind of cop-out, it's a true-blue zombie attack that not only actually happens to the characters, but serves as a focal plot point for the rest of the season. Plus, best buddies Troy and Abed frequently act out childish fantasies—and I don't mean childish as in immature, I mean childish as in the kind of blissfully unashamed fun most adults only *wish* they could have. While the network execs haven't always understood what was so great about *Community*, we, the fans, do—it's why we've all clung to the phrase uttered by Abed on one simple episode: "six seasons and a movie!"

Sokka

*"Each of you is so amazing, and so special. And I'm ... not.
I'm just the guy in the group who's ... regular."*

While much of *Avatar*'s story focuses around Aang and Zuko, there's still a strong supporting cast. You've got the maternal Kotarra, hard-headed Toph, slyly wise Uncle Iroh, and, of course, Sokka. Sokka provides much of the show's comic relief, but he's far more than a bull's-eye with "Punchline" written across him. Whereas the rest of the cast wield awesome supernatural powers, Sokka lacks such preternatural abilities. Similar to *Buffy*'s Xander, he struggles with feeling unskilled and useless. Ultimately, he manages to persevere by doing some soul-searching and discovering what he's good at. Whereas many shows would be content to make Sokka useful by handing him a magic sword and calling it a day, *The Last Airbender* makes him *work* for what he gets. This goofball puts in a lot of effort to get from point A to point B, and he serves as a great example for everyone struggling to figure themselves out. The moral? Being special isn't something you're given, it's something you *earn*.

Seven Geek Characters Who Could Really Use a Friend and a Hug

7 | **The Ice King** – *Adventure Time*

6 | **King Dedede** – The *Kirby* series

5 | **Edward Scissorhands** – *Edward Scissorhands* (make sure it's a careful hug)

4 | **Zoidberg** – *Futurama*

3 | **Frankenstein's Monster** – *Frankenstein*

2 | **Heero Yuy** – *Gundam Wing*

1 | **Akuma** – The *Street Fighter* series

Fractured fairy tales aren't anything new—characters such as Cinderella and Snow White have existed for *centuries,* so it's not surprising that writers will come up with new, updated takes on them. *Once Upon a Time* provides one such take. This multi-faceted fantasy program takes familiar fairy tale characters and plays with them in oh-so devilish of ways, like by making Little Red Riding Hood a friggin' *werewolf.* Producer Adam Horowitz said of the show, "The idea is to take these characters that we all know collectively and try to find things about them that we haven't explored before. Sometimes it's a story point, sometimes it's a thematic connection ... We are not generally retelling the exact same story as the fairy tale world."

Once Upon a Time maintains a fairly healthy budget, giving the audience plenty of special effects shots of the enchanted fairy tale land, magical birds, or a buttload of dwarves. The show alternates between Storybrook's "real world" and the fairy tale world, which helps keep things feeling fun without risking *Batman and Robin*-level hokeyness ... although *Once* isn't afraid to take risks. Storylines frequently wrap up with the show's status quo chewed up and spit out like gristle—*Once Upon a Time*'s first concern is telling an engaging story, no matter how much hell it puts the writers through. People constantly become enchanted/get amnesia/get super amnesia and/or die, which keeps the suspense pumping week after week. And, with the show's theme of fractured fairy tales (and liberal access to the library of Disney tales and characters), you never know *who* you're going to see next.

Warehouse 13 is about a secret government warehouse that collects supernaturally-charged artifacts and stores them away from the untrained hands of the common folk.[30] While the premise firmly embeds this show in the fantasy genre, *Warehouse 13* manages to take something fantastic and somehow make it feel scientific. Most every artifact, from Lewis Carroll's looking glass to Marilyn Monroe's hairbrush, somehow ties back to true-blue people in history. Sure, Lewis Carroll may never have *really* had a mirror that can trap your soul, but, based on his outlandish and occasionally frightening body of work, the existence of such an artifact makes sense. Not only do these items provide fun excuses for the *Warehouse 13* gang to get into all sorts of shenanigans, they also teach the viewer snippets about (mostly) real historical figures.

While the hunt for dangerous artifacts provides the fuel for the show's fire, its amazing characters will keep you crowded around it. Lead characters Pete and Myka have a brother-sister bond based on mutual respect, rather than the often trite romantic tension to which most shows default to. Warehouse expert Artie was quite the badass in his day and now that he's a bit older, he manages to somehow be both cuddly and curmudgeonly. And few characters can pull off the one-two-three punch of hilariousness, intelligence, and likeability you'll find in Allison Scagliotti's performance as Claudia Donovan. The entire cast is great, from the main-est of main characters to the briefest of guest stars.

Each season has some sort of over-arcing story to deal with, but the bulk of most episodes is devoted to the characters contending with whatever the artifact of the week is. This particular pacing makes it easy for someone to drop in on any given episode, while at the same time rewarding long-time fans with the addition of little nods and gags to previous adventures. And while many shows are content to be sourpusses, *Warehouse 13* thumbs its nose at such melodrama. Every character has their moments of comedy, helping to keep things feeling light and fast-paced no matter what the situation is.

---

[30] Remember the warehouse from the end of *Raiders of the Lost Ark*? *Warehouse 13* is basically about that.

Eight Mythical Characters We Need to See on *Once Upon a Time*

8 | **Character**: Gilgamesh
Storybrook alter ego: A samurai swordsman with a penchant for sweets and a dog named Enkidu.

7 | **Character:** Mushu the dragon
Storybrook alter ego: A fast-talking grifter looking for his next deal.

6 | **Character:** Glooskap
Storybrook alter ego: A biologist/wildlife specialist who prefers to spend his days outdoors and fights to protect the environment.

5 | **Character:** Pockets, that fat kid from *Hook*
Storybrook alter ego: A fat kid.

4 | **Characters:** Flotsam and Jetsam, the eels
Storybrook alter ego: Two dim-witted thugs with heterochromia.

3 | **Character:** Doctor Facilier, the Shadow Man
Storybrook alter ego: An evil-ass voodoo witch doctor.

2 | **Character:** Simba
Storybrook alter ego: An actual friggin' lion.

1 | **Character:** The Gnome-Mobile
Storybrook alter ego: An RV piled to the rafters with lawn gnomes.

MEDIEVAL FANTASY: +5 VORPAL BLADES FOR EVERYONE!

There's a reason you don't see many shows set in anything other than modern eras: it's expensive, and no matter how diligent you are, there's *bound* to be an anachronistic goof or two that slips in. That didn't deter the creators of *Hercules: The Legendary Journeys, Xena: Warrior Princess,* or the more recent fantasy show, *Game of Thrones*, from having a go at it. Long before Sam Raimi was directing your friendly neighborhood *Spider-Man* or wowing people with the wonderful wizard of *Oz*, he was re-imagining Greek mythology with a distinctly '90s flair. Both Xena and Hercules make for great protagonists; they're wise, sexy, ready to throw down if necessary ... and Xena has more than a little red on her file to make up for. Both shows had solid runs of half a decade or more, and while their tones may have oscillated wildly from slapstick to melodrama, it doesn't change the fact that they're so bursting with heart and enthusiasm, you'd be remiss not to give them a look.

Game of Thrones, however, doesn't lean toward the fun as much as its two Greek-inspired forebearers. In fact, you'd be hard pressed to find much "fun" in any given episode of *GoT*, except, perhaps, for the rare instances in which we get to see King Joffrey take a slap to the face. Based on George R.R. Martin's as-of-yet unfinished *A Song of Ice and Fire* book series, *Game of Thrones* combines complex storytelling with myriad characters and a general sense of brutality. If you're thinking of letting the kiddies hop on the train to adulthood and watch some more mature television, this probably shouldn't be their first stop—it might traumatize the poor buggers. And of all the fantasy worlds you could let them experience, Westeros is one of the harshest, *filthiest* ones around.

GETTIN' SPOOKY WITH IT: SCARY SHOWS

"You are about to enter another dimension ... a dimension not only of sight and sound, but of mind." That's right, bitches, you're entering *The Twilight Zone*. The 1950s aren't exactly known for being the most free-spirited of eras. During that time, pretty much everything awesome—free thought, imagination, sexuality—was suppressed with an iron grip and a feigned smile. But in spite of these constraints, *The Twilight Zone* stepped in, wreathed in its dark tales of morality, and dismissed the status quo with a wave of its

The Top Ten Ways to Die in a Filthy, Medieval World

10 | By the sword.

9 | Getting burned at the stake for being a witch.

8 | Inadvertently attending the Red Wedding.[31]

7 | Trusting other people.

6 | Supernatural monster, such as vampires, witches, or super-witches.

5 | Death by cooties.

4 | Something simple and totally preventable, like a mild fever, that medieval doctors were too primitive and stupid to treat correctly.

3 | Child birth.

2 | Death by poison.

1 | Death by Roger.

---

[31] Never, never RSVP to a Red Wedding.

black and white hand. Clichéd family fantasies like *Father Knows Best* and *Leave it to Beaver* have crumbled into irrelevancy under the ravages of time and cultural advancement, but the balls-out originality of *The Twilight Zone* keeps it firmly ensconced as an important piece of pop culture.

Much of *The Twilight Zone*'s success can be attributed to its creator/host Rod Serling. He framed each *Twilight Zone* episode with a bit of exposition and waxing philosophic. As our voyeuristic guide to each disquieting tale, he was dignified, but with a hint of melancholy, as if he regretted being unable to step in and help the poor saps of the week from getting sucked into their fates. It's not all bad, though, because, while many fantasy/horror anthologies are content to make bad things happen to people at random, *The Twilight Zone* typically reserved its judgment for those who bring such punishment upon themselves.

The Twilight Zone's special effects aren't anything to write home about nowadays, but its content and emotional/philosophical core have remained mostly intact. Plus, the show is so seminal that there are moments which continue to be referenced in popular culture to this day, such as the cruel godling Bill Mumy's unyielding rule in "It's a Good Life," William Shatner's impassioned duel with the airplane-obsessed gremlin in "Nightmare at 20,000 Feet," or the twist reveal of Donna Douglas' beauty and the hideousness of her doctors and nurses in "The Eye of the Beholder."

The Outer Limits fits into that same groove as *The Twilight Zone*, but since *The Twilight Zone* is the senior-most show in the "spooky, moral anthology series from the late '50s and early '60s" genre, this newcomer just didn't catch on the same way. Maybe because its theme song isn't as catchy, or it doesn't have a host as engaging and well-dressed as Rod Serling, or maybe it's because it doesn't have an episode featuring a malevolent doll named Tiny Tina.

The Twilight Zone and *The Outer Limits* feature a lot of monsters, but ask anyone who knows a thing or two about the black beasts and they'll tell ya that monsters should be the ones that are afraid. Why? Cause the Winchester brothers are on the case, and they're looking to send more than a couple creepy crawlers straight back to Hell. *The X-Files*, *Buffy the Vampire Slayer*, and even *Smallville* all utilized the "monster of the week" format to ensure that trouble keeps flowing in for our beloved protagonists week after week. *Supernatural*, however, too that trope and celebrated it, giving us the weekly exploits of the Super Winchester Bros., Sam and

Five Artifacts *Warehouse 13* Should Have Featured

5 | **King Leonidas' Loincloth**

Ability: Grants unparalleled combat abilities, strategic acumen, and six-pack abs.

Drawback: The constant, almost overwhelming urge to shout things and kick people into pits.

4 | **Sherwood Schwartz's Glasses**

Ability: Fills the wearer's mind with ideas for countless hit television shows.

Drawback: Also fills the wearer's mind with the theme songs to *Gilligan's Island* and *The Brady Bunch;* it's like background music, only you can't change what songs are playing, adjust the volume, or ever turn it off.

3 | **Stan Lee's Typewriter**

Ability: Gives you great power ...

Drawback: ... but also great responsibility.

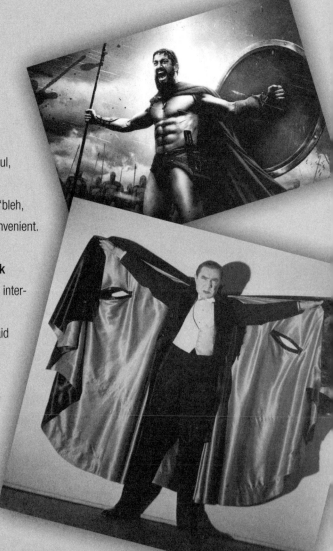

2 | **Bela Lugosi's Cape**

Ability: Grants the wearer a powerful, hypnotic stare.

Drawback: The wearer has to say "bleh, bleh, bleh" whenever it's most inconvenient.

1 | **George R.R. Martin's Desk**

Ability: The ability to craft complex, inter-weaving stories.

Drawback: The inability to *finish* said complex, inter-weaving stories, and the desire to talk about food and slaughter your characters like some kind of food-obsessed Jason Voorhees.

Dean, as they traverse the continental U.S. (which in no way resembles Canada) on their quest to gank the baddies and keep the goodies alive.

The Winchester brothers get embroiled in some pretty complicated family drama. They fight with each other, they fight with their dad, they fight with each other *about* their dad, and they generally end up throwing down with every other Winchester they ever stumble across during this non-stop road trip. Their weekly battle to banish ghosts, slay sasquatches, and lock up Lucifer may not be something most folks can relate to, but that ongoing problem of family squabbling sure as hell is.

Throughout history, people have imagined numerous creepy, crawly things that go bump in the night, and *Supernatural*'s got an open casting call for all of them. Sometimes the monsters are things we've all heard of, such as zombies, non-sparkly vampires, and demonic gophers. Other times the creatures are lesser known, with beasts like Lamia and Rakshasa stirring up trouble. Even the commonly known creatures have imaginative spins put on them. Take the djinn, for example. While they're more commonly known as wish-granting genies, on *Supernatural*, they put their victims into dreamy, happy little comas where they *think* their wishes have come true, and while their victims snooze, the djinns make a slow snack out of them.

Supernatural ain't shy about stacking up the bodies. People die a lot on this show, and they die in truly awful ways. Any given episode probably opens with a shriek, a splash of blood, and the title screen slapping you in the face like a pillowcase stuffed with old batteries. The show isn't all death and destruction, though; there's a grim sense of humor in pretty much every episode. Dean Winchester digs the kind of jokes you'll hear from cops, soldiers, and ER doctors—a dark brand of comedy known as the "gallows humor" or a "graveyard sense of humor." He also tempers his graveyard jokes with a double dosage of sarcasm and a go-to-hell, never-say-die attitude. To help things stay fresh and not get *too* gloomy, some episodes break the horror format entirely in favor of comedy, like the sitcom-themed "Changing Channels," where a powerful Trickster locks the Winchesters into enacting surreal, TGIF-esque shows. At more than a hundred seventy episodes, there's a *lot* of time to be spent onboard the S.S. Supernatural, so once you've decided to hop aboard, know that you can kick back, relax, and enjoy a hellacious ride with these two badass bros.

Top Ten Television Science Fiction/Fantasy Badasses

10 | **Ace Rimmer**[32] – *Red Dwarf*

9 | **Starbuck** – *Battlestar Galactica* (2004)

8 | **Xena** – *Xena, Warrior Princess*

7 | **Captain Kirk** – *Star Trek: The Original Series*

6 | **Daryl Dixon** – *The Walking Dead*

---

[32] What a guy!

Those Wacky Undead

Should a zombie outbreak occur, if given the option between being bitten and becoming a zombie or continuing to fight for some scrap of survival in the world of *The Walking Dead*, I think I'd rather go zombie. *The Walking Dead* is rough with a capitol *rip you in half and eat your guts.* Beloved characters die horribly. Psychotic villains live far longer than they should. Carl won't stay in the damn house. Based on Robert Kirkman's comic of the same name, AMC has a smash hit on their hands with this show about carnivorous corpses, and for season after season, viewers keep tuning in to find out who will survive, as well as vicariously living out their own zombie outbreak fantasies. *The Walking Dead* may be rough, dirty, and quite un-sexy, but it still makes for a hell of a zombie-drama.

5 | River Tam – *Firefly*

4 | Dean Winchester – *Supernatural*

3 | Spike Spiegel – *Cowboy Bebop*

2 | Sayid Jarrah – *Lost*

1 | Sarah Connor – *Terminator: The Sarah Connor Chronicles*

True Blood, on the other hand, is *sexy*. *True Blood* seems perfectly at home on HBO, where it can be free to pack every episode with all of the delightful nakedness that nearly everyone wants to see, but might not admit to wanting. *True Blood* makes full use of this freedom by having its cast of good-looking, incredibly fit actors rock it *au naturale,* and rock it quite often. *True Blood* provides eye candy of all flavors, so no matter what you're hungry for, you'll find it.

Sexiness aside, *True Blood*'s a pretty damn dark show. In addition to the frequent softcore boobs and butts, you'll also find two scoops of hardcore violence. People get dismembered, decapitated, and disemboweled. When vampires get staked, they don't turn into the neat little piles of dust—they explode into eruptions of gore. Viewers with weak stomachs may need to look elsewhere, and those looking for something purely on the sexy side may want to look into getting Cinemax instead. It's all very over the top, but what do you expect from a show about vampires, fairies, djinns, weird lust goddesses, werewolves, werepanthers, werehorses, and weremacaroni and cheese? *True Blood* has the unique position of being uniquely *True Blood*— every episode has occurrences that couldn't happen anywhere else, with characters who could only live in Bon Temps, Louisiana.

Here are some more shows that center around beings who, while technically deceased, don't let that stop them from living life to the fullest: *Being Human, The Vampire Diaries, Forever Knight, Pushing Daisies, Desperate Housewives.*

SPACED-OUT SHOWS

Space. Some say it's the final frontier. Personally, I think the *real* final frontier is what gas station bathrooms taste like—that's something *nobody* wants to explore. Still, the vastness of space provides a lush setting for exploration. There's so much unknowable wonder out there that the best we, as humans, can do is write television shows set in outer space and hope for the best.

Star Trek has always been about boldly going where no one has gone before, whether it's through stories of otherworldly cultures, goatee-bearing evil twins, or Captain Janeway and Lieutenant Paris getting turned into lizards in the darkest and dumbest of all episodes. You see, *Star Trek* is so much more than a show about a bunch of goobers flying around in space; it's a progressive bit of pop culture about the importance of

True Blood's Top Five Best Characters

5 | Alcide Herveaux

4 | Jessica Hamby

3 | Jason Porkhouse

2 | Lafayette

1 | Seriously, Lafayette's the best. Nelsan Ellis kills it as this charismatic, good-hearted guy with a penchant for eye makeup and calling everyone, living or otherwise, on their baloney.

peace, the search for knowledge, and the acceptance of other cultures.

J.J. Abrams' *Star Trek* flicks may lean more toward lens flares and action, and while Shatner's Kirk was predisposed toward throwing punches and seducing green ladies, no matter what version of *Star Trek* you're watching, its heart remains the same. Good science fiction uses its stories of scientific craziness as a way of holding up a mirror to society and helping us make sense of it. The Federation may assign ships to fly around in space, but it's for the sake of exploration and understanding, not to scout out (see also: steal) resources, or swipe other races' technologies. *Star Trek* may be science fiction, but underneath the transporters and phasers it's a sociological examination of the human condition.

Captain Kirk

"KHAAAAN!"

The original captain *loved* the ladies and wasn't afraid to settle things by throwing a punch or bashing the Gorn in the belly with a rock. He was equal parts lover, fighter, and philosopher. Chris Pine's modern take on Kirk blends the humor and charm of Kirk with the ruggedness of Indiana Jones, while Shatner's portrayal of the character will be forever remembered for the *Stuttering! Ex ... clamatory Way He Would ... Often Speak!* He'll also be remembered for his impassioned kiss with communications officer Uhura.[33] The sight of an interracial couple kissing is no big deal nowadays, but back in the original *Star Trek*'s era, this vanilla-on-chocolate sexiness caused quite a stir. NBC asked that the scene be filmed with an *implied* kiss rather than a real one, but Shatner and Nichols conspired together to "flub every take," so that NBC had no choice but to run the scene as intended.

First-Hand Geekiness: *Star Trek*

When *Star Trek: The Next Generation* premiered, I was 8 years old. My dad was very excited for the premiere, and that made *me* excited. Watching that show would be the birth of a life-long love of Sci-fi. To my child's mind, here was an amazing, magical show where anything could happen. They had a magical play place in the holodeck.

---

[33] Nichelle Nichols' Uhura is a legend in her own right, as she was one of the first African-American characters to be portrayed on TV in a non-menial role.

Strange-looking aliens were integral to the show. You never knew what amazing thing they would encounter next week.

More than that, I loved Deanna Troi. Growing up in a small town in West Texas, I witnessed casual misogyny every day, even at my young age. In elementary school, I was already battling with a society that considered boys to be stronger, tougher, and smarter. In PE, I wanted to play soccer with the boys, but they would openly ignore me and never pass me the ball. The PE coach didn't understand why I didn't just hang out in the shade and braid my hair with the other girls. I was a very smart tomboy, but was made to feel inferior because I wasn't pretty like my female classmates. Even the teachers made me feel like I was too smart, and should probably not be so obvious about always knowing the right answer. I wasn't too young to see the annoyance on everyone's face every time I raised my hand. I didn't understand what I was doing "wrong" because my parents encouraged me to be myself.

Once per week, I would watch *Star Trek: The Next Generation*. Tasha, of course, was tough and smart. Beverly was brilliant and an excellent caretaker of the crew on the ship. But Deanna, a beautiful woman (whose beauty was rarely remarked upon and not once used as a tool), was a trusted advisor to the incredible Captain Picard. She was a bridge officer simply for her ability to perceive, understand, and empathize with others; that had a powerful impact on me.

For me, at such a young age, to see a woman in a powerful, trusted position, not in *spite* of her "feminine" qualities but *because* of them—that affected me in a way I wouldn't truly understand until many years later.

I will always be grateful to *Star Trek: The Next Generation* for giving me seven years of weekly lessons in not giving up, always making use of the gifts you're given in life, and NEVER trusting a Ferengei, no matter *what* they say.

— Jessica Mills
Creator and star of the geeky webseries A*wkward Embraces*
@geekyjessica

Geeky Influences: *Star Trek*

The amazing thing about geeks is that one good geek can beget another. Gene Roddenberry created *Star Trek*, and his little show had an enormous enough impact to inspire future geeks into all sorts of directions.

The creation of Mary Sues, slash fiction, shipping, and fan fiction in general. In the '60s and '70s, hungry *Trek* fans took to their typewriters and notepads to create new *Star Trek* scripts in the hopes that their lovingly crafted story might grace the glow of their television screen some day. Time and time again, the writers over at *Star Trek* found that these fan-written stories revolved around a new ensign, often female, who had recently been assigned to the Enterprise and yet was better than everyone at the things they were normally good at—they'd beat Bones at medicine, out-logic Spock, and crush Kirk's skills of diplomacy.

Skim the surface of the internet and you'll undoubtedly find gallons of fan fiction simmering like the contents of a pot of overly enthusiastic chili. Some fans enjoy focusing their thematic efforts on the romantic elements of a show, imagining what it

Five of the Worst *Star Trek* Episodes Ever to Curse This Earth With Their Presence

5 | **"The Paradise Syndrome"** – *Star Trek: The Original Series*
Kirk gets amnesia and joins a tribe of Native Americans. Actually, I think this episode crosses the line from "dumb" into "so dumb it's awesome."

4 | **"A Fistful of Datas"** – *Star Trek: The Next Generation*
The official episode description? "Due to a computer malfunction, Worf, Deanna Troi, and Alexander Rozhenko get trapped in an Old Western holodeck program where all the characters look like and have the same abilities as Data." I almost feel that this goofy-ass script was the result of a lost bet or something, like maybe Brent Spiner beat somebody at a game of beer pong, and because of it, they had to film the most ridiculous premise he could think of.

3 | **"And the Children Shall Lead"** – *Star Trek: The Original Series*
Let's see, character development? Nope. Suspense? Nada. *Any*thing interesting or original about the episode? Doesn't seem so. Obnoxious little know-it-all children? Oh hell yes, it's got *loads* of those. Shatner over-acting? You better believe it. "The worst the script, the more I over-acted," he once said, and after watching this episode, it's hard not to believe him. Most Trek fans decry

would be like if two characters hooked up.[34] Kirk and Spock were one of the earliest, and most popular, instances of the fandom shipping two characters together, inspiring future fans to pair together any two characters that tickled their fancy in what's called "slash fiction," with pairings such as Legolas/Gimli, Megatron/a toaster, or The Doctor/himself.

Starbase Dental. In Orlando, Florida, a *Star Trek* superfan took it upon himself to remodel his dentist's office with the aesthetics of a Federation ship. It's a beautiful sight, almost enough to make you forget that there's a dude about to drill a hole in your head.

Klingon rock bands. Death metal. Klingons. Two tastes that combine as naturally as peanut butter and bumpy-headed peanut butter. The band's five founding members, Bill

"And the Children Shall Lead" as being the worst of the original series, and it's hard to argue to the contrary. Even other not-so-good episodes such as "The Savage Curtain" had crazy stuff like Abraham Lincoln showing up to help keep things appealing, but this has absolutely nothing to keep people's interest—almost a feat within itself.

2 | **"Let He Who is Without Sin"**– *Star Trek: Deep Space Nine*
While this episode was supposed to be a thoughtful examination of sex in the twenty-fourth century and how it reflects our own modern sensibilities on the topic, since the writers weren't able to actually *show* much of anything relating to sex, the whole thing feels like a fifth-grade sex-ed video shown to you by your mom and narrated by Ben Stein.

1 | **"Threshold"** – *Star Trek: Voyager*
Poor Brannon Braga. You write a zillion episodes, which all go without a hitch, but then you come out with a single bafflingly bad script and it's all anyone can remember you for. Of course, when it's as bad as "Threshold," you deserve to take some heat for it. The science behind Warp 10 turning Janeway and Paris into lizards is totally-batcrap-loco-wrong, and then they mate and have lizard babies? Only in bad fan fiction should we get stuff this weird.

---

[34] A process known as "shipping."

Salfelder (*plnluH HoD*), Merlin Carson (*Che'ron muchwI'*, Ward Young (*KhR'ELL*), Jason Lewis (*Khraa'Nik*), and Jason Johansen (*Qui Pe*), formed a death metal band named after the Klingon afterlife. They sing songs in Klingon, they dress as Klingons onstage, and each have a Klingon name. Suffice to say, these dudes friggin' love them some Klingons.

The creation of cosplay. Cosplay wasn't always the booming and popular pastime it is today; years ago, fans wouldn't think of dressing up as their favorite characters. In stepped the Trekkies,[35] the only group bold enough to say, "Hey! I totally dig Captain Kirk, and I'll be damned if anyone's gonna tell me I can't dress as him for conventions and whatnot!" After wetting their feet with *Star Trek* cosplay, fans began branching out. We got *Star Wars*, *The A-Team*, even *CBS Evening News with Walter Cronkite* cosplay. Today, you can find any and everyone at a convention, with the more creatively minded fans finding new ways of representing their beloved heroes and villains.

Most younger science fiction fans won't be familiar with *Lost in Space*, or the god-awful movie starring Matt Leblanc and that girl from *Mean Girls*, but the impact of the Space Family Robinson's adventures can be felt even today. Sure, *Lost in Space* was

Battlestar Galactica's Top Five Greatest Adama-isms[36]

5 | "Use the frakking razor, you fool!" – Season four, episode two, "Adama Gets a Haircut"

4 | "Not in my backyard!" – Season one, episode thirteen, "Boomer's Bonzo Beach Party"

3 | "I'd like to sell tickets to *that* dance." – *Battlestar Galactica: Razor*

2 | "So say we all." – Pretty much every episode.

1 | "Shaky shaky bong bong!" – Season two, episode twenty, "The Admiral's New Catch Phrase"

---

[35] Also Trekkers, Trekzillas, and Trekkamundos.
[36] Two of these are real Adama-isms, and the rest are … less than real. I'll leave it up to you to suss out which is which.

technically a science-fiction show, but in actuality, its stories often delved into fantasy rather than science fiction. Creator Irwin Allen was more interested in telling broad stories appealing to young and old than he was in making any sort of commentary on society, and it's reflected in the show's frequent bouts of fantastical kitschiness.

But not all sci-fi is content to camp out in Camp Campiness; 2004's reimagining of *Battlestar Galactica* takes its stories *seriously*. This re-imagining of the original '70s series took the original mythology and explored it at length, often taking the show into wild new directions. Fans are still a bit divided about its ending, but it's difficult to argue that you didn't get seventy-five episodes of intensity. The cast is also another strong point, with Tricia Helfer as the scheming Number Six, Mary McDonnel as the stressed-out President of Frakking Everything, James Callis as the brilliant (and somewhat crazy) Gaius Baltar, and, of course, Edward James Olmos as Commander Adama.

While a lot of sad stuff happens on *BSG*, fans can find solace in the fact that it got to tell its story to its conclusion ... which is more than *Firefly* ever got.

No other program is as brief and belovedly tragic as Joss Whedon's *Firefly*. Both the show's setting and its behind-the-scenes story are soaked in gooshy poignancy. *Firefly*'s story centers around a group of rebels, smartypantses, and, well, Jayne, all drawn together because of various failures and problems in their lives. Most of them have suffered loss and disappointment at the hands of The Alliance, the powerful governmental body insistent on unifying the universe, regardless of whether they care to be unified or not. Though Mal and his crew were the plucky underdogs who fought the good fight, ultimately, they lost and were left with little choice but to keep their heads down and try to make their way through the 'verse. Similarly, Joss Whedon had a specific vision for *Firefly*, and he clashed with the powerful FOX executives over it constantly. Ultimately, FOX pulled the plug fast and hard because they were short-sighted wang chungs.

It's unfortunate, too, because, in addition to *Firefly*'s wonderful setting, its characters were fully-formed from the get-go. While most shows have to feel out the dispositions of their characters for a while, trying to figure out which actor is best suited as the funny one, the broody one, or the one obsessed with hamburgers, *Firefly*'s nine leads seemed bred for their specific roles, and slid into them naturally from the very first episode.

Though the show was short, we did get *Serenity*, a theatrically released follow-up that provided some small measure of closure.[37] And let's not forget the countless ways in which Firefly has influenced us since its departure.

---

[37] Mostly in the form of Joss Whedon killing off a few characters. Again. Curse you, Whedon! CURSE YOUUUU!

Geeky Influences: *Firefly*

Firefly's cancellation served as a unifying force across the geek 'Verse. It united fans, both in our outrage over its unjust cancellation, and in our continuing hope that it might, someday, return to the small screen. Suddenly, we weren't merely fans of the show, we were the rebels fighting back against pig-headed powers that be. As time passes, most fans have outwardly moved on to other things. Inside, however, there's still a little part of us that will always wear brown.

Jayne's hat. In "The Message," Jayne dons what might be the sweetest piece of headgear ever to grace a television screen: an orange and yellow knitted cap that basically looks like a piece of candy corn. "A man walks down the street in that hat, people know he's not afraid of anything," reasons Wash, who can only look on in what I'm sure is awe at the

GEEK
Spotlight

Captain Malcolm Reynolds

"I aim to misbehave."

Good ol' Mal is a complex guy. He's broken-down, but never busted; noble, while simultaneously ignoble; he's as tenacious as they come, but most of all, he's freaking cool. He's both noble and ignoble, and he's about as tenacious as they come. This war vet's seen far too much action for one man. Now all he cares about is seeing that he and his crew survive to the next day. According to the man himself, actor Nathan Fillion, Mal's crew is as much a reflection of himself as they are their own people. "In Wash, he has a lust for life and a sense of humor he's lost. In Jayne, he has selfishness. In Book, he has spirituality. In Kaylee, he has innocence. Everybody represents a facet of himself that he has lost and that's why he keeps them close and safe, and yet at arm's length."

majesty of Jayne's hat. This goofy little cap has become a popular item at conventions across the 'Verse. Everywhere you look, you'll find people wearing the hats, selling the hats, or making their own. Though FOX has tried to crack down on the "unlicensed" manufacturing/selling of this beloved item, it'll never stop *Firefly* fans. You can't stop the signal, and you can't stop Jayne's hat.

For more shows about characters who are lost/living in space, check out: *Space Cases* (created by *Lost in Space*'s Bill Mumy), *Star Trek: Voyager, Star Trek: Deep Space Nine, Star Trek: Enterprise, Babylon 5, Blake's 7, Red Dwarf, Josie and the Pussycats in Outer Space,* and the surprisingly good *Captain Simian and the Space Monkeys.*

Space Madness

Here are some short-lived space/future-themed shows that may not have lasted long, but they made up for their brevity by (mostly) not being very good: *Far Out Space Nuts,*[38] *Homeboys in Outer Space,*[39] *Galaxy High, C.O.P.S, Partridge Family 2200 A.D., Space Cases.*[40]

TIMEY WIMEY SHOWS

It would be abso-flipping-lutely insane to begin any discussion of time travel shows without covering the granddaddy of them all: *Doctor Who*. This British icon has intrigued audiences for fifty years—and counting! For the three of you out there who aren't familiar with the good Doctor's exploits, he's a time-traveling philanthropist. Armed with only his wits, a handy-dandy sonic screwdriver, and a vessel capable of transporting its passengers through time and relative dimensions in space (otherwise known as a TARDIS), the Doctor flits around the universe from beginning to end and back again, helping people (and aliens), and inspiring those around him to be bigger and better than they ever thought they could be. There aren't many fictional characters who've become so globally recognized as this madman-in-a-box, and part of the reason

---

[38] Which is essentially a show about Gilligan and the Skipper lost in space, right down to Bob Denver starring as the skinnier, dopier of the two.

[39] Which is essentially a show about Gilligan and the Skipper, if they were black and in space.

[40] I'll give *Space Cases* some credit: it's way better than the other shows on this list. Still, if you go back and watch it as an adult, you'll see that there's duct-tape holding the friggin' show together. Sets are cheap, most of the kid actors seem distracted, and the '90s special effects are *'90s special effects.*

Popular Variations of Popular Characters

Pirate version. How to do it: add a pirate hat and bandolier to your costume. Bonus points for sporting an eyepatch and spouting a healthy "Gyarr!" every second or third sentence.

Zombie version. How to do it: put on some bloody makeup.

Steampunk version. How to do it: throw gears and goggles on friggin' everything.

Gender-swapped version. How to do it: dress as if your character is the opposite gender he/she normally is. Bonus creativity points if you're the character's default gender, but swap anyway, like if you're male and dress as a female Aquaman.

is, despite the Doctor's extraordinary nature, he taps into some of our most buried, most childish, most *important* wishes: to do good and to *explore*.

"When you run with the Doctor, it feels like it'll never end. But however hard you try, you can't run forever. Everybody knows that everybody dies and nobody knows it like the Doctor. But I do think that all the skies of all the worlds might just turn dark if he ever for one moment, accepts it. Everybody knows that everybody dies. But not every day. Not today. Some days are special … Now and then, every once in a very long while, every day in a million days, when the wind stands fair, and the Doctor comes to call … everybody lives."

-River Song
"Forest of the Dead"

First-Hand Geekiness: *Doctor Who*

Doctor Who shouldn't have worked, really. It's intended to be family programming but deals in high-concept science fiction and has a body count in almost every story. It's an action hero who refuses to carry weapons most of the time and often has his plans fail, at least at first. It has no static setting, cast, or premise. But instead of failing, it has only grown and expanded, creating multiverses that can be grim or hopeful. You can tell any story you want with *Doctor Who* and then tell it again from a different angle. That's fantastic.

-Alan Kistler
Author of *Doctor Who: A History*
@SizzlerKistler

Geeky Influences: *Doctor Who*

Increased amount of crossplay.[41] Go to any convention and you'll find more cosplay than ever before, and more *creative* cosplay than ever before. Imaginative fans have become increasingly unfettered by the concept of "race" or "gender" when it comes to dressing up as their favorite characters. All across the convention floor, you'll see African-American Captain Americas, Caucasian Black Lightnings, and, of course, female Doctors. The Doctor's various incarnations all have very distinct outfits which tend to look good on a person regardless of gender— helping encourage any and everyone to dress up as their favorite Doctor, whether it's Ten, Two, or Eleven with a fez.

Increased sci-fi fandom of all shapes, sizes and creeds. Though *Doctor Who* typically has a cast of about two— the Doctor and his (typically female) companion— this tight, tiny team helps the show feel approachable for any and everyone. Similarly, the secondary characters are often impressively varied, not only in terms of gender balance, but also of ethnicity and sexual orientation, giving you the feeling that *Doctor Who* is not a show aimed at a particular type of person, it's a show aimed at *people*.

---

[41] Cross-dressing + Cosplay. Women dressing as male characters, and men dressing as female characters. Hey, if you love Storm, don't let that Y chromosome keep you from dressing as her! And if you're a lady who is way into *Duke Nukem*, Nuke it up, yo!

Though some shows featuring superpowered characters don't have them showing off the good stuff in order to keep the budget down,[42] *Terminator: The Sarah Connor Chronicles* said "to hell with that!" and gave us the good stuff start to finish. Any given episode will probably have several shootouts, car chases, and maybe even a little terminator vs. terminator brawling. It's a pricey show, but the creators made every penny count, and because of that, we never get an episode that seems constrained by budgetary issues.

For most of the series, we've got three primary leads: Cameron (the terminator), John Connor, and, of course, Sarah Connor. Far from the whiny anarchist we saw in *T2, Sarah Connor Chronicles'* John Connor is a moody, heroic, traumatized mess of a kid. He'd probably qualify for post-traumatic-stress disorder if he could ever get to that *post* stage of stress instead of being perpetually embroiled in it. A lesser actress would probably have screwed up in her portrayal of terminator Cameron. After all, if she showed too much emotion she wouldn't be believable as a robot, and if she didn't show enough, the audience wouldn't be able to connect with her. Somehow, though, Summer Glau balances out this tightrope of emotion perfectly and makes us care about this surreptitious killing machine. As Sarah Connor, Lena Headey manages to bring out the duality of being a vigilant soldier and a compassionate mother, all while looking kickass in a black jacket.

Don't expect to see any episode descriptions with stuff like "John considers the finer points of crochet" or "Cameron has to go on two dates in the same night without letting either of her dates know." This smart show respects you, the audience, enough to treat you with the intelligence you deserve. Its episodes are complex affairs that weave together an over-arcing story through the use of multiple 45-minute tales of terminator-induced woes.

Though *T:SCC* is a show about cybernetic assassins, time travel, and philosophical determinism, beneath its metal exterior beats a human heart. As mentioned before, you really grow to care about these characters, and that's because the show gives you time to get to know them and root for them personally. Sure, there's the larger mission to save the world from destruction at the hands of killer robots, but ultimately it's about a mother fighting to ensure her son sees a better tomorrow, a son trying to figure out who he is, and a machine struggling to connect with others.

Should your heart desire more television shows with a time-traveling flair, check out: *Quantum Leap, Red Dwarf, Time Tunnel, Primeval, Fonz and the Happy Days Gang,[43] Life*

---

[42] I'm looking at you, *Heroes.*

[43] Of course. The logical cartoon spin-off of a show about a bunch of teens in Milwaukee is to have it be about them traveling through time with a chick from the future.

on Mars, the *Peabody's Improbable History* segments on *The Rocky and Bullwinkle Show*, *Time Squad, SuperBook, DuckTales, Histeria!, Voyagers!*, and, of all things, *Felicity*.

While the ratings monster that is *Lost* left a fanbase divided over its finale, it's hard to argue with the ambition or success of this ABC sci-fi drama. It had a massive, diverse cast, storylines with more twists and turns than a minotaur's maze on acid, and a gorgeous setting—it's a show about an island, after all, and creators J.J. Abrams, Jeffrey Lieber, and Damon Lindelof made damn sure it was filmed on one. Why settle for a sterile Hollywood backlot when you could instead have the luscious greens of the Aloha state?

Lost's cast was *huge*. Any given episode could have upwards of a dozen important characters interacting with each other. With a cast so large, you'd think it would be difficult to make sure everyone gets their moment to shine, but *Lost* is as much about each character's journey as it is about its ongoing story. In a typical episode of *Lost*, you'll get half present-day antics on the island and half flashbacks to

GEEK Spotlight

Gyro Gearloose

The exploits of *DuckTales'* most prolific inventor can also double as a cautionary tale for every excitable geek out there: finish what you start. While all of Gyro's inventions are brilliant, many lack some key feature needed to make the damn thing safe or usable, all because Gyro got so excited about moving on to his next project that he forgot to *finish the first one.* Any of you geeks hard at work on your novel, tabletop game, or sex dungeon, keep working until the job's done! An unstable sex swing helps no one.

the past of whomever was most important that week. Framing each episode that way was a bold choice, but it paid off. and as a result, we get plenty of glorious, in-depth growth for each of our beloved Losties, getting to see who they are, how they became that way, and where they're going.

Lost is a mystery wrapped in an enigma ensconced in a conundrum and baked into a fortune cookie. Watching it you'll find that questions keep flitting through your mind like confused bumblebees.

"What's the deal with the malevolent smoke monster?"

"Why are the Dharma Initiative people running all those damn tests?"

"What's up with the hieroglyphics?"

You'd need a journal to keep track of all the threads of mysteries happening on that

GEEK
Spotlight

Velma

"Jinkees!"

Oh, Ms. Dinkley, how you ensnare my heart with your brain. It's true that *Scooby-Doo* is about a group of mystery-solving teens and their talking dog,[44] but without the efforts of that orange-clad brainiac, they'd all probably be in Shaggy's basement playing Monopoly.

---

[44] For all the mysteries Mystery Inc. solves, they never bother looking into the biggest mystery of all: why can Scooby-Doo and his entire canine family talk? Nobody ever bats an eye at these talking dogs, and yet they don't really cross paths with *other* talking dogs. What gives?

island, and that's part of the appeal. Audiences would tune in, week after week, to see if they'd finally get sweet release from the questions that had been plaguing them long ... but if you have yet to experience *Lost*, know this: some answers will be found, and will satisfy you to your core. Others will not and will haunt you to the end of your days.

THE ART OF MYSTERY

Lost's mysterious mythology provides a large part of its appeal. If you're looking for more shows hinging on pervasive weirdness and ongoing enigmas, check out: *Twin Peaks, Pretty Little Liars, The Fugitive, Tru Calling, Carnivàle, The Event, Revolution*, and for a couple of good, geeky detective shows, there's also *Monk, Psych*, and *Scooby-Doo* in its many forms.

Ten Mysteries, Events, and Occurrences That Set the *Lost* Fandom's Blood Boiling

10 | What's with the polar bears?

9 | What's with that giant statue's foot?

8 | Where'd Jack's dad's body end up?

7 | Seriously, what's with the damn polar bears?

6 | Libby's unceremonious death.

5 | Why is Kate so ridiculously good-looking?

4 | Why is the episode about Jack's tattoo so god-*awful*?

3 | The way Rose would always say Barnard's name as *"Bernerrrrd."*

2 | Nikki and freaking Paulo.

1 | Waaaaaaaaaaaaaaaaaalt!

CORPORATE CRAZINESS

As humanity progressed through the 20th century, we, as a species, moved away from working outside and toiling in the fields like a bunch of damn donkeys to instead stay primarily indoors, clacking away at our computers like a bunch of damn donkeys with fingers. This change in business culture changed our popular culture, leading to the following funny, wacky, corporately themed shows that poke fun at how soul-sucking corporate jobs can be: *The IT Crowd, Better Off Ted, The Drew Carey Show,* and *Dilbert.*

ANIME[45]: WITHOUT IT, YOU'D ALREADY BE DEAD

Animation can make for a wonderful medium when trying to tell larger-than-life stories. If you want to see a show about people who pilot gigantic robots in massive, Helm's Deep-level engagements every episode, it's probably not going to be live action. It'd be too costly, would probably look silly, and where would everyone keep their giant robot suits when they're not filming? For most of their history, American animated shows were thought of as for kids, covering simple issues all while trying to entice the little rugrats to buy toys.

In Japan, however, their animated shows will often veer into more adult territory, covering exciting things like ninja battles, demon rituals, and The Devil's part-time job. Japanese anime excels at telling the kinds of stories that would be difficult in other mediums and frequently uses jaw-dropping animation techniques you won't see anywhere else. While many consider anime a genre of television, in actuality, it's more of a multi-genre conglomeration. There are all different types of anime, some focusing more on political commentary and the horrors of war, and others focusing on teams of magical girls who transform into even more magical girls to fight monsters.

Several seminal programs helped increase anime's popularity across the globe, with *Cowboy Bebop* in particular being a big influence in the rise of anime in America over the last decade. *Bebop*'s adventures of Spike, Jet, Faye, Ed, and Ein mish-mashes themes of existentialism, noir, and nihilism. It had a limited run of twenty-six episodes and a movie, which was exactly the way creator Shinchiro Watanabe wanted it. *Bebop's* clean, precise story gets precisely to the point it wants to make without flitting around and, oh, I don't know, killing time by having Spike power up into Super Spike for an entire episode, unlike *Dragon Ball Z.*

---

[45] Japanese anime was invented in 1997 by a German man named Gustav Gunter. Well, that's what he tells everyone, anyway.

Top Eleven TV Geeks

11 | Liz Lemon – *30 Rock*

10 | Chuck Bartowski – *Chuck*

9 | Henry Deacon – *Eureka*

8 | Comic Book Guy – *The Simpsons*

7 | Maurice Moss – *The IT Crowd*

6 | Claudia Donovan – *Warehouse 13*

5 | Samuel "Screech" Powers – *Saved by the Bell*

4 | Willow Rosenberg – *Buffy the Vampire Slayer*

3 | Sheldon Cooper – *The Big Bang Theory*

2 | Abed Nadir – *Community*

1 | Steve Urkel – *Family Matters*

The *Dragon Ball* saga, including its precursor, *Dragon Ball*, and follow-up, *Dragon Ball GT*, is mostly known for muscular men yelling, shooting laser beams at each other, and punching the bejeezus out of anything that moves. There's a bit more depth to *DBZ* than that, but, admittedly, not much. *DBZ* has a lot of fluff to it, content to spend full episodes doing things such as the aforementioned powering up, or watching Goku try to get his driver's license, or everyone just standing around while glowering at each other. Much of *DBZ*'s appeal is in its execution of its villains. Folks like Cell and Majin Buu aren't merely bad, they're evil and downright obnoxious. Watching these nigh-invincible psychopaths episode after episode is enough to make you furious, but when the baddies finally get their comeuppance, they get it *hard*. A measure of a good villain is how satisfied the audience feels in seeing him/her go, and few things are as satisfying as watching a psychotic, muscle-bound murderer get vaporized by a totally badass Kamehameha beam.

FIVE HUNDRED EPISODES? SOUNDS GOOD TO ME.[46]

For more anime that follows the *Dragon Ball Z* formula of spending plenty of time pooting around (and subsequently giving you a lot of episodes to enjoy) check out the

---

[46] For anyone who feels like getting technical, you'll notice that I'm not breaking down every show based on its variant names, like *Naruto: Shippuden, Gundam: Wing,* or *Yu-Gi-Oh! GX*. That's because there's too damn many name changes for all of these shows, so if I listed them all, the list would have become fat, boring, ugly, and had a dumb-looking haircut.

The Seven Dumbest Rejected *Dragon Ball Z* Villains

Akira Toriyama had a thing for naming his characters after food, hence we get food-themed *Dragon Ball* characters like Vegeta (vegetable), Piccolo (pickle), Gohan (Japanese for rice), and Launch (lunch). Those who weren't named explicitly after food often had puns to their monikers, like Frieza and his entire chilly family. These kind of naming conventions can be cute, but there's a point where it's *too far*, which is probably why these losers ended up on the cutting room floor.[47]

7 | **Nap** and his brother **Kin,** two titanic bald guys who obsess over cleanliness.

6 | Vegeta's super evil brother, **Froot.**

5 | **Sahn, Muhn,** and **Stohrz,** three aliens hailing from the planet Plahnit.

4 | **Toyl,** and his boss, **Lit,** two aliens who constantly make bathroom puns.

3 | Launch's sisters, **Deena** and **Breakfast.**

2 | **Steve, Steve,** and **Steve.** Under a time constraint, Toriyama suggested that the next villains to attack the Z-Fighters be three unrelated guys with the same name.

1 | **Potato,** a large tuber with arms and legs. He fights using sumo wrestling techniques and cannot speak other than screaming the word "potato."

following: *Sailor Moon, Bleach, Slayers, Inuyasha, Naruto, First of the North Star, Yu Yu Hakusho, Ranma 1/2, Voltron: Defender of the Universe, Robotech, Gundam,* and *One Piece. Yu-Gi-Oh!* and *Pokémon* both fit the bill, too, though they're a bit different in that they're also maniacally engineered to get you to spend your hard-earned buckos.

And, if you're in the mood for some anime that gets to the point a little more quickly, check out: *Star Blazers, Full Metal Alchemist, Space Battleship Yamato, Ghost in the Shell, Wolf's Rain, S-Cryed, Gurren Lagan, Guyver, Soul Eater,* and *Evangelion.*

---

[47] I think these guys are all made up, though it's been a while since I've watched *Dragon Ball Z*, so I could be wrong.

Ten TV Shows Insidiously Designed to Trick You into Buying Cards, Toys, Video Games, and Whatever Else They Can Think of

10 | *Pokémon*

9 | *Yu-Gi-Oh*

8 | *Transformers*

7 | *The Centurions*

6 | *Bey Blade*

5 | *Bakugan*

4 | *Lego Ninjago*

3 | *GI Joe*

2 | *He-Man and the Masters of the Universe*

1 | *The Golden Girls*[48]

---

[48] Come on, after watching an episode of *Golden Girls*, who doesn't feel the urge to run out and buy a Betty White with Karate Chop action figure, or a Bea Arthur with Removable Shoulder Pads of Destruction?

SUPER MEN, WONDROUS WOMEN, AND OTHER HEROIC BEINGS

Most know superheroes as stars of the silver screen and the ink-stained pages of comic books, but there are more than a few television shows dedicated to superpowered so-and-sos running around helping others.

Wonder Woman was among the earliest television programs to focus on, as *Heroes* was so fond of calling them, a "person with abilities." While Diana Prince may not get the multimedia coverage she deserves today, it doesn't change the fact that, in the '70s, *Wonder Woman* beamed into living rooms all across America, showing young would-be heroes a badass chick with a knack for getting the truth, deflecting bullets, and fabulous accessorization. Linda Carter's performance as Wonder Woman balanced out coyness and grace. Sure, she'd save you, but she'd take a second to crack a one-liner while she did it.

GEEK
Spotlight

Major Motoko Kusanagi

"I mean, have you ever actually seen your brain?"

Who knows what the future will be like, but if it resembles the one depicted in *Ghost in the Shell*, it's going to be dangerous and filled with electronic threats and existential crises. While cybernetic implants are common in Motoko's age, she's gone whole-hog by becoming a fully synthetic being. It may be handy not having to worry about mortal stuff like aging or eating too many cookies, but Motoko's transformation has left her often questioning whether she was ever *actually* human, or if she's only ever been a ghost-in-the-shell. As far out as Motoko's internal crisis may seem, as technology advances, it's probably going to be an issue many of us face: to stay simply human, or become something more, something *super.*

Not wanting to be left out in the rain, Marvel created its own superhero show: *The Incredible Hulk*. *Hulk* combines elements of classic Westerns, with their wandering heroes doling out justice, and, of all things, werewolf mythology. Mild-mannered David Banner[49] transforms into the Hulk and smashes stuff whenever needed ... and whenever it was most inconvenient. Bill Bixby brings some gravitas to Banner, making it easy for the audience to root for him, while Lou Ferrigno's performance as the Hulk often channels the essence of that big kid on the playground who wants to play rough. He's not bad, per se, and he'll cool it if there's something really wrong, but he'd *much* rather smash a sandcastle than build one.

Later on, we got *Lois & Clark: The New Adventures of Superman*. Sure, the show is now so '90s it borders on painful, but the strength of Teri Hatcher and Dean Cain's performances as Lois and Clark, respectively, helped keep it fun even when the scripts got dumber (and boy did they). Later on, the WB revisited the Superman mythos from a younger angle with *Smallville*, telling the story of a teenage/young adult Clark Kent on his journey to go from super boy to Superman. The show ran for approximately seventy-two thousand years, and after it finished, the WB—now reforged as the CW—brought forth *Arrow*. It may be a young show, but it has potential. Though *Arrow* spends most of its time obstinately refusing to call Green Arrow by his right name, it does bring a *Dark Knight*-esque gritty realism to TV superheroes, and makes clever use of DC's roster of supervillains.

For a while, *Heroes* seemed destined to be a franchise people talked about for years to come ... and I guess people still do, although not for the reasons creator Tim Kring probably wishes they would. After a stellar first season, the world demanded to see more of the adventures of Peter Petrelli, Claire Bennet, Hiro Nakamura,[50] and the rest. But then season two came along, and three, and four, each with its own problems. Season two was too slow. Season three was gonads-out crazy. Season four's heart just wasn't into it. That's not to say that the last three years were a total wash, but *Heroes* never

---

[49] I know his name's Bruce Banner. On the TV series, however, it was David, because the network told Stan Lee they thought Bruce was an effeminate name. Why? Because TV executives are morons, who are almost always wrong about everything.

[50] Oh, *I* get it! His name is Hiro, and he wants to be a superhero on the show *Heroes*! HOW FREAKING CLEVER!

Ten Superheroes Who Need Their Own Modern Live-Action Shows

10 | Daredevil

9 | Batgirl

8 | The Flash

7 | Luke Cage and Iron Fist: Heroes for Hire

6 | Black Canary

5 | Doctor Strange

4 | Zatanna

3 | Ultimate Spider-Man—Peter Parker or Miles Morales.

2 | Wonder Woman—handled by anyone who *didn't* create Ally McBeal.

1 | Batman

again managed to come close to the complex goodness that was season one.

If you're hankering for more television superhero action, here are some more shows for your eyes and earholes: *The Greatest American Hero, Misfits, Birds of Prey, Kamen Rider/Masked Rider, Mighty Morphin' Power Rangers* and its many variations, *Blade: The Series, Black Scorpion, M.A.N.T.I.S,* and *The Flash.*

And, for some great animated superhero shows that will appeal to both young and old, check out: *Young Justice, Batman: The Animated Series, X-Men, X-Men: Evolution, Freakazoid, Ben 10, The Spectacular Spider-Man,* pretty much any version of the *Teenage Mutant Ninja Turtles,* and three shows that are a bit more ironically entertaining than they are legitimately entertaining, *He-Man and the Masters of the Universe, She-Ra: Princess of Power,* and *Super Friends.*

SCIENCE GONE MAD

Like a mischievous puppy dog, science doesn't always do what we tell it. Sometimes it gives us the cure to a disease; other times it makes a huge mess in the Large Hadron Collider without even telling anyone. While this sort of scientific jack-assery is annoying and dangerous in real life, on television it makes for glorious entertainment, as evident by *Eureka*, a show about a secret town filled with the world's greatest scientists and the everyman sheriff who has to keep these eggheads from accidentally nuking themselves.

STEM—Science, Technology, Engineering, and Mathematics. These four things are among the most important passions we humans could devote ourselves to. It's through research into STEM subjects that we discover new things about ourselves, about life, the universe, and everything! One of the many things that sets *Eureka* apart from other academically minded shows is that few programs celebrate geeky passions like STEM the way Eureka does. Over and over again, you'll see

GEEK Spotlight

Fargo

Sheriff Carter: *"What button'd you push this time?"*
Fargo: *"Can you not recognize a victim when you see one?"*

Fargo's genius is never in question—he's brilliant in pretty much every field, from physics to A.I. What is questionable, though, is his tendency toward accidents, belligerent behavior, and his general inability to let things go. More than a few "incidents" at Eureka are because of Fargo pushing a button he wasn't supposed to or butting heads against one of his many, many rival scientists. Sure, he's immature, but, at the end of the day, his lovable nature shines through, ensuring that the people around him don't strangle him after surviving whatever daily mishap he's incited.

how awesome being a nerd is and the kinds of awesome stuff you can do if you put your mind to it. You can invade people's dreams! Visit parallel timelines! Make really good coffee! Science is awesome, and great shows like *Eureka* help encourage young fans to grow up to create more science-y awesomeness.

STEM aside, *Eureka*'s just a damn good show. Actor Colin Ferguson has a strong background in comedy, and it shows in his performance as Sheriff Carter, the relatable guy amidst the unrelatable craziness. He brings an enthusiastic energy you don't get from most television leads, helping keep viewers entertained even as the other characters spew technical (and occasionally dry) science-y wience-y stuff.

Often science and academically minded shows are total white sausage-fests, but *Eureka* defies the odds with its large cast of diverse people. Too frequently we see writers forget that heterosexual white males aren't the only ones in the universe. Also, like Syfy's other mega-hit, *Warehouse 13*, *Eureka* knows when it's time to put on plot pants, and when to take off them plot pants off and show that comedy underwear. Though each season has an over-arcing story to it, with the later seasons having especially interesting plots, there's a hefty amount of comedy to go along with it. Sheriff Carter's constant bewilderment to the scientific insanity around him is always good for some laughs, as is his daughter, Zoe, and her snark-ariffic teen snappiness, or the eccentricities and rivalries of the many academics around town. Geeks may get stereotyped as being a timid lot, but *Eureka* shows that they're clearly not, with none as surprising in their belligerence as Douglas Fargo.

While *The X-Files* isn't the first show to introduce a new problem every week, it was among the first programs to sling a new monster to investigate each week, breaking ground for other shows like *Buffy the Vampire Slayer* and *Smallville* to follow suit. Some things about *The X-Files* are subtly '90s (just check out Scully's shoulder pads) but for the most part, it ages surprisingly well.

David Duchovny absolutely kills it as Fox Mulder, whose brilliant eccentricities make him a joy to watch episode after episode. (He's so good, in fact, that the two Mulder-less seasons really seem to drag without him). He has plenty of quirks, like how readily he believes in the paranormal and his habit of leaving porn casually on in the background while he's working, but, in addition to that genius weirdness, he also has a wry sense of humor and an unbridled enthusiasm for his work, because, as Mulder puts it, "The truth is out there."

Scully, on the other hand, isn't quite so eager to embrace the supernatural as her partner, which is why she ends up having the larger character arc of the two agents. Initially, she's the skeptic, always countering Mulder's paranormal theories with her

Nine of the Most Unbearably Bad Movies Made Watchable Thanks to *Mystery Science Theater 3000*

9 | **Film:** *Time Chasers*
Highlight of the Episode: The main villain shoots and kills the hero, and then a bit of fuselage falls on him, slaying him as well. After a moment of contemplation, Mike appreciatively says, "Oh, *well*. Thank you, movie."

8 | **Film:** *Hobgoblins*
Highlight of the Episode: As a jacket-clad goober tries ineffectively to sneak alongside a wall, Tom caresses our ears by singing a few lines from A-Ha's *Take On Me*.

7 | **Film:** *Laserblast*
Highlight of the Episode: When Mike and the bots discover that legendary film critic Leonard Maltin gave Laserblast 2-1/2 stars, they go through the rest of his film book to see how this flick about a whiny teen-turned-caveman/alien with a laser arm stacks up against other, actually *good* 2-1/2 star movies.

6 | **Film:** *Future War*
Highlight of the Episode: *Future War's* never-ending supply of fake-looking cyborgs and even faker-looking dinosaurs.

5 | **Film:** *Warrior of the Lost World*
Highlight of the Episode: *Warrior of the Lost World's* smarmy, A.I. infused motorcycle that won't shut the hell up.

logical (a.k.a. less cool) ideas. But she can only maintain that skeptic's armor for so long, and whenever something weird happens, we see a twinge in her eye betraying the crack in her armor. Ultimately, after *far* more evidence than it should take, Scully goes full-on believer. But when Mulder disappears, she gets paired with Robert "Have You Seen This Boy" Patrick, leaving her in the position of being the believer trying to convince her skeptical partner of the truth.

4 | **Film:** *Horror of Party Beach*
Highlight of the Episode: *Horror of Party Beach's* cheesy monsters, whose appearance suggests they tried to stuff as many pickles in their mouths as possible before proceeding to terrorize the beach-dwelling teens.

3 | **Film:** *The Wild Wild World of Batwoman*
Highlight of the Episode: After several minutes of the characters inexplicably partying (despite the fact that the film's main storyline was wrapped up quite some time ago), Tom has enough, and screams, "END! EEEEEEND!" with a rage unlike any living being before or since.

2 | **Film:** *The Final Sacrifice*
Highlight of the Episode: Nothing in *The Final Sacrifice* can measure up to the awesomeness of world's most magnificent drifter—Zap Rowsdower!

1 | **Film:** *Space Mutiny*
Highlight of the Episode: There's *so* many great things about this episode, but of particular note is the way the guys constantly produce new nicknames for *Space Mutiny's* barrel-chested, strong-chinned hero: Slab Bulkhead, Fridge Largemeat, Smash Lampjaw, Punt Speedchunk, Butch Deadlift, Blast Hardcheese, Thick McRunfast, Buff Drinklots, Splint Chesthair, Bold Bigflank, Flint Ironstag, Bolt Vanderhuge, Crunch Slamchest, Fist Rockbone, Stump Beefknob, and Rip Steakface.

Man, *Futurama* really is the little show that could, isn't it? It has gotten revived more often than Professor X, thanks to its incredibly loyal fan base and passionate, intelligent creators. Voice actor for Fry/Zoidberg/Farnsworth/about a billion other people, Billy West, had this to say about the writing: "It had more layers than an onion. These writers meant business. There was a level for everybody. Your major could be celestial mechanics, and there'd be celestial-mechanics jokes."

Futurama doesn't talk down to you, which is more than I can say for other, less cognitively taxing shows such as *King of Queens, Duck Dynasty,* or *Guess Who'll Get Voted Off Next,*[51] the more you know and the more you pay attention, the more you'll get out of watching *Futurama.* This show is really, truly funny, not just funny the way you say your homely friend is "funny" because they don't have anything else going for them, and it's thanks to the show's bizarre sense of humor, which gave us such great gags as the Grunka Lunkas, Snoo Snoo, and HYPNOTOAD.[52]

Mystery Science Theater 3000's concept is so ingeniously simple that many who saw it probably smacked themselves in the head for not thinking of it first. Ever since video rentals came into existence, we've had groups of similarly minded snarkypants renting cheesy movies for the sole purpose of talking over them. *MST3K* takes the noble art of riffing on films and elevates it to new levels. Mike (originally Joel), Tom Servo, and *Croooooow!* save us the trouble of locating terrible movies and provide us with hours of entertainment as they sit and watch these atrocities, armed only with their razor-sharp wits and pop culture references. It's easy to riff on movies as awesomely terrible as *The Room, Plan 9 From Outer Space,* and *Troll 2,* but with nigh-unwatchable horrors such as *Manos: The Hands of Fate*, it requires real skill to elevate them to comedy gold.

Ahh, *Family Matters.* If you remember the show, you might remember the early seasons, back when it was about a lower-middle class Chicago family? Well, few shows go so off the freaking rails from their base concept as this Miller-Boyett production, and it's all thanks to pesky-neighbor-turned-mad-scientist Steve Urkel. Later seasons brought us such scientific anomalies as

---

[51] *Guess Who'll Get Voted Off Next* is a reality competition without any actual competition. Contestants live out their regular lives for the cameras and then show up to a warehouse once a week. The viewers then get to vote on who gets to go home and who has to metaphorically go home by getting kicked off the show. The winner gets a slap in the mouth and a gift certificate to the Olive Garden.
[52] ALL GLORY TO THE HYPNOTOAD.

Steve Urkel

"Did I do that?"

The sitcoms of the late eighties and early nineties were formulaic, to say the least. Nearly all of them had a blowhard father, know-it-all younger sibling, and annoying neighbor who won't go home. *Family Matters* began with a family, but lacked that special pest-next-door. .. until Steven Q. Urkel appeared in a puff of smoke and cheese. Urkel quickly became the focus of the show, thanks, in no small part, to Jaleel White's ability to take otherwise horrendous scripts and perform them with gusto. Few television characters are as iconic as Urkel, with his suspenders, bright striped shirts, nasal speech, and copious catch phrases. Years from now, after human civilization has been turned to dust in the great psychic dog apocalypse of 2173, neo-humans will find what's left of our culture and see the one called "Urr-kill." Though they may not know "Urr-kill," deep down, somewhere in their DNA, they'll hear the echoes of those four words long since uttered: *Did I do that?*

Ten Ways in Which Most People Would Abuse Time Travel

10 | Only paying for an all-you-can-eat buffet once, and then swapping out with yourself every time you want a meal.

9 | Trying out pick-up line after pick-up line on a hottie by going back in time and redoing it whenever you mess things up.

8 | Slapping the bejeezus out of Hitler.

7 | Making tons of money abusing the stock market.

6 | Trying to kidnap Bill Cosby.

5 | Giving wedgies to a childhood bully.

4 | Warning your younger self about future embarrassing moments, like that fateful afternoon when you chowed down on a bunch of cookies and juice, spent too long in the hot sun jumping on a trampoline, and then proceeded to vomit your body weight in blue fruit punch and Keebler cookie fragments.

3 | Harassing famous historical figures while they're trying to write the speeches, fight the battles, and invent the inventions that make them famous.

2 | Stealing important artifacts like Ben Franklin's kite or Buzz Aldrin's jockstrap.

1 | Trying to record a video of the Big Bang so they can post it on Facebook, Twitter, Instagram, or HellzYeahScientificAnomalies.Tumblr.

Urkel bots, Jekyll/Hyde transformation potions, time travel, teleportation devices, and shrinking/growing rays. Perhaps what is most (unintentionally) hilarious about these events is how nonchalantly everyone handles them—patriarch Carl Winslow has the same annoyed reaction to Urkel inventing a time machine as he does to his son asking him for more money.

For more shows about the hazards of insane super-science, check out: *Fringe, The Venture Bros, Jonny Quest, Inspector Gadget, Teenage Mutant Ninja Turtles,* and *Dollhouse.*

THE BIGGEST STINKERS OF THE GEEK SHOW WORLD

Not every show can be great. With the light, comes the dark. With good, comes evil. With *Doctor Who* comes *Star Cops.* Geek show stinkers include*: Heroes* (after the first season), David E. Kelley's *Wonder Woman* pilot, *Total Recall 2070, Manimal, The Powers of Matthew Star, Mercy Point, Space Precinct, Tekwar, Krod Mandoon and the Flaming Sword of Fire,* and *Poochinski.*

THEY'RE HERE TO SAVE THE WORLD.

BILL MURRAY   DAN AYKROYD
SIGOURNEY WEAVER

GHOSTBUSTERS

COLUMBIA PICTURES PRESENTS
AN IVAN REITMAN FILM
A BLACK RHINO/BERNIE BRILLSTEIN PRODUCTION
"GHOSTBUSTERS"
ALSO STARRING HAROLD RAMIS   RICK MORANIS
MUSIC BY ELMER BERNSTEIN "GHOSTBUSTERS" PERFORMED BY RAY PARKER, JR. PRODUCTION DESIGN BY JOHN DE CUIR
DIRECTOR OF PHOTOGRAPHY LASZLO KOVACS, A.S.C. VISUAL EFFECTS BY RICHARD EDLUND, A.S.C. EXECUTIVE PRODUCER BERNIE BRILLSTEIN
WRITTEN BY DAN AYKROYD AND HAROLD RAMIS   PRODUCED AND DIRECTED BY IVAN REITMAN

PG PARENTAL GUIDANCE SUGGESTED
SOME MATERIAL MAY NOT BE SUITABLE FOR CHILDREN

ORIGINAL SOUNDTRACK ALBUM ON ARISTA RECORDS

DOLBY STEREO
IN SELECTED THEATRES

Chapter 3

Movies:

Books for Your Eyes and Earholes

Getting into a new television series can be hard. The earliest episodes of any show are often the roughest, but they also tend to be required watching if you want to understand what's happening once things finally pick up. You're risking a lot when you invest time into a show—once things *do* finally get good you may not know whether you actually enjoy what you're watching, or if you only think it's good because you're suffering Stockholm Syndrome due to the being held hostage by this crummy show for so damn long. Movies, however, provide a quick, clean enjoyment. A good movie doesn't require a 10+-hour time investment[53] and gives you every juicy bit of detail you need to enjoy what's happening on-screen. Plus, since moviemakers don't have to worry about keeping costs down over the span of several seasons, a lot of movies are expensive, gorgeous affairs, like piñatas stuffed with diamond-encrusted candies.

---

[53] Unless it's a Judd Apatow flick, because that dude's movies are *always* too long.

Super Men, Wondrous Women, and Other Heroic Beings: The Movie

Superhero flicks are among the most expensive types of movies being made right now—with great power, comes a great special effects budget. But our favorite caped crusaders weren't always the multimedia powerhouses they are today; for most of their history, comic book characters were considered "kid stuff" by the public at large. In 1978, it took a whole team of writers, directors, and producers to find the right way to bring *Superman*'s iconic story to life on the big screen. Once Christopher Reeve slipped into the role, however, the man's natural talent made the rest of the filming process a cakewalk. It's hard to think that fifty-five million dollars was enough money to bring such a super-powered hero to life, but director Richard Donner and his team made it work, resulting in a box office smash and several sequels—one that was awesome, one that was not so good, and one that was stupendously terrible.

It was over a decade before we'd see another major superhero film, but in 1989, Tim Burton was called in to help create the film *Batman*. His star, Michael Keaton, seemed a strange choice for such a powerful character, given his background in comedy, but he suited Burton's vision of Batman as a guy who became something more than just a man when he put on the suit. Jack Nicholson was a natural fit for the Joker, bringing a real sense of both menace and superficial joviality, and the score from Danny Elfman is among film's most iconic—many later iterations, including the amazing *Batman: The Animated Series*, also make use of it. Though some elements of Burton's *Batman* may seem odd to those familiar with the character,[54] this moody, action-packed flick put booties in seats and lead to a series of sequels.

Though *Batman* was a fairly straightforward tale, *Batman Returns* is a bit of a mess. There's plenty of fantastic imagery, with the same hellish, gargoyle-laden Gotham of the first film, but these positives easily get lost in a muddled plot and overly large cast. Like bacon, adding Christopher Walken enhances nearly anything, but in *Batman Returns*, his character detracts from time that could have been spent with Michelle Pfeiffer's purr-tacular Catwoman, or Devito's grotesque Penguin.

Batman's third theatrical outing, *Batman Forever*, wants to get into people's heads. Dr. Chase Meridian (Nicole Kidman) is *way* into Batman. "Why does he go around punching bad guys, wearing a cape, and looking so cool?" she wonders as she doodles bat-shaped hearts signed CM + BM. Luckily for her, Bruce Wayne's bat-skills haven't been so focused lately, so he approaches the good doctor to help him reach the man beneath the cowl ... without letting her know *too* much, of course. Batman can't go

---

[54] Why on Earth does Batman go around killing random henchmen? He's got a pretty strict policy about that kind of thing, you know.

around telling everyone his secret identity or it'd just be his *regular* identity. But with her help, he works through the sadness and guilt he feels over his parents' untimely demise, helping bolster his resolve to be the best Batman he can be.

While Dr. Meridian metaphorically traipses around people's minds, the Riddler does it literally. Tech geek and all around weird dude Edward Nygma doesn't understand others, but he does understand their *brains,* and he invents an iRiddle streaming device which lets people experience TV and movies as never before, all for the small cost of unwittingly allowing Nygma to rummage around in their memories like a garage sale enthusiast who shows up awkwardly early.

Between Tommy Lee Jones' one-sided portrayal of Two-Face and director Joel Schumacher's penchant for pulsating laser lights, there's little subtlety to *Batman Forever*, but you'd be hard-pressed to find a film more unshakably enthusiastic. And sure, *Batman Forever* veers pretty heavily into cheesiness sometimes, but for the most part, it keeps the *gravitas* and goofballiness[55] balanced out, unlike its follow-up, *Batman & Robin*, a flick so aggressively awful it would destroy superhero films for nearly a half-decade.

---

[55] Yes, that's a real word. Wait, are you about to look it up? Don't you trust me?

Ten Things That Suck About *Batman & Robin*

10 | Why would Batman put nipples on his costume?

9 | The Bat-Credit Card.

8 | Mr. Freeze's ludicrous addiction to ice-related puns.

7 | George Clooney's ho-hum performance as Batman. Can you imagine him trying to deliver some of the Dark Knight's most iconic lines? "I'm vengeance. I'm the night, I guess. (shrugs) I'm Batman."

6 | Director Joel Schumacher attempting to copy the campiness of the '60s *Batman* series and instead taking a dump all over everything and everyone.

5 | Barbara's "Uncle" Alfred makes her Batgirl costume ... so why is it so sexy and form-fitting? That's not creepy at all.

4 | Pretty much everything about Uma Thurman.

3 | Gotham's overabundance of neon lights. Gotham City isn't a 24-hour rave, *Schumacher*.

2 | Bizarre, Hanna Barbera-esque sound effects at inappropriate moments.

1 | Mr. Freeze, a character confined to a cryogenic suit because his body can't survive normal temperatures, smokes a cigar. That's the same as a normal person chugging a milkshake made of freaking *lava*. The only reason those cigars are even in there is because Arnold Schwarzenegger, who got paid a smooth *twenty-five million* to be in this garbage heap, loves cigars so much he wanted to smoke them as part of his character. Maybe some of that Arnold money would've been better spent on, oh, I don't know, writing a better script?

Thanks to *Batman & Robin*, DC's superhero flicks had to sit on the sidelines for a few years so the general public could recover. Marvel brought the new millennium in with a bang with *X-Men* in '00 and *Spider-Man* in '02. Both films were such successes that they lead to a ton of sequels and made stars out of pretty much everyone involved, such as Anna "Don't Call Me Sookie" Paquin, Hugh "Sure, You Can Call Me Logan, Mate" Jackman, and James "Why The Hell Was I on *General Hospital*?" Franco. Both *X-Men 2* and *Spider-Man 2* built on the themes and characters of their predecessors and managed to surpass them in pretty much every way. *X-Men 3* and *Spider-Man 3,* however, were a bit less successful and a bit messier.

GEEK
Spotlight

Tony Stark

"Let's face it, this is not the worst thing you've caught me doing."

An egocentric, genius billionaire playboy philanthropist isn't exactly the most *relatable* of characters, but somehow Robert Downey Jr.'s performance as Iron Man taps into the element that made the character so interesting in the first place: his heart.

Sure, he spends most of his time being an egomaniacal ass. Most people would in his situation—he's rich, talented, and had success handed to him on a gilded platter. But beyond all of the money and ego, Stark wants his gifts to be used to help other people; seeing them misappropriated and used maliciously drives him out of his selfish little shell and into the metallic shell we all know and love.

After Marvel's properties started raining money, DC finally got back in on the action with Christopher Nolan's *Batman Begins*. It's not uncommon for comic book heroes to undergo "dark and gritty" reboots, but in this case, grounding Batman in a moody, semi-realistic setting was precisely the shot in the arm the Caped Crusader needed. *Batman Begins* eschewed the flashy weirdness of previous Batman iterations in favor of focusing on Bruce Wayne's pursuit of justice in a world gone gritty. It also revamps Batman's origin to include some ninja training, which now puts him firmly on the side opposite pirates in the age-old Ninjas vs. Pirates debate. Like both the *X-Men* and *Spider-Man* trilogies before it, most consider the second entry, *The Dark Knight*, to be the best of the Nolan Batman films, and the third entry, *The Dark Knight Rises*, to be a bit on the uneven side.

If you're reading this book, chances are you've seen *The Avengers*, and probably more than one of the movies building up to it. Marvel directly funded *Thor, Captain America: The First Avenger,* and *Iron Man* thanks to the sizable bankroll they made off of their previous films. For years Marvel's movies have been on a unstoppable rollercoaster of box office obliteration—and for good reason. Iron Man, Thor, and Captain America all manage to tell different kinds of superhero stories, and, thanks to sharp directing, writing, and performances, make you care about heroes you probably weren't all that interested in before. Captain America's always been too clean-cut for most people, and Thor is bit too old-school. And Iron Man? Before Robert Downey Jr. stepped into those mechanical shoes, you'd be hard-pressed to find a comic book fan who would list the character as his/her favorite hero. Nowadays you'd have to work harder to find someone who *doesn't*.

If you're looking for more cinematic superhero shenanigans, check out: *The Incredibles, Man of Steel, The Punisher,*[56] *Ghost Rider, The Crow, The Shadow, The Mask, Fantastic Four, Darkman, The Rocketeer, Mystery Men, The League of Extraordinary Gentlemen, Hellboy, Sky High, Hancock, The Guyver,* and the many sequels most of these films have.[57]

Close Encounters of a Lovable Kind

It's a sad fact that most movies featuring extra-terrestrial intelligence depict aliens who are more interested in seeing what our insides look like than they are in hanging

---

[56] The 2003 iteration starring Tom Jane, not the terrible Dolph Lundgren version.

[57] But for the love of all that's good and holy, don't watch *Son of the Mask*—that piece of trash should be nuked from orbit.

out at Starbucks and grabbing a half-caff-venti mocha. There are some flicks, however, which depict alien life with varying degrees of relatability. We may be from different planets, but that's no reason we can't all get along.

Will Smith

"Welcome to Earth."

Punches alien in head and then lights cigar.

"Now that's what I call a close encounter."

Few people have the raw charisma to pull off a one-liner, let alone a *double* one-liner,[58] but by *God*, Will Smith did it. While it may seem funny to think of the Fresh Prince as a major contributor to science fiction, if you go back through most of his filmography you'll find that he's spent most of his film career avoiding aliens, manhandling massive machines, and rough-housing with robots. His movies aren't always the most contemplative take on their source material (and many of his later projects are, at best, lifeless affairs like *Men in Black III,* and, at worst, boring, nepotistic affairs like *After Earth*). Regardless of the thoughtfulness of his filmography, though, these flicks help expose a wider audience to geekiness, inspiring some to further explore things such as artificial and extra-terrestrial intelligence, which is always a good thing.

---

[58] Known in the United Kingdom as a two-liner, in Canada as a double looney, and in France as a royale with cheese.

According to *Men in Black*, deep down, every being in the universe is just a schlub who wants to make his/her/its way through life. *MIB* also twists up the buddy cop genre by combining sci-fi alien hijinks with the genre staple of having two disparate heroes team up to fight the baddies. Given that the quality of a buddy cop film lives and dies on the quality of its two leads, it's a good thing, then, that *MIB* brought in Will Smith and Tommy Lee Jones, both of whom were at the top of their game. Smith has his usual affable charm as streetwise Agent J, and Jones delivers his dialogue with a stone-faced sarcastic flair. The clever combination of CG and traditional effects help *MIB*'s special effects hold up where other CG blockbusters haven't aged so well.

Like *Men in Black*, *District 9* depicts aliens who just want to get by. The Prawns have some sharp-looking technology, but most of them don't seem to know how it works—in much the same way that, if you ask a random layperson how a microwave functions, he or she would have no idea. These bug-eyed beings don't seem all that different than us, which is probably why we treat them so badly. In much the same way that South Africa's Apartheid system segregated and mistreated black people, here we see the Prawns being treated the same way, highlighting the horror and absolute injustice that occurs over there to this day.

If you've seen *The Fifth Element*, you'll know that there's something ineffably strange and heartfelt about it. Its depiction of the future is simultaneously glamorous and ignoble; calloused, yet caring; and so very, very odd. There's a lot to love in this weird duck of a movie, starting with the fifth element herself, Milla Jovovich. Her performance as Leeloo Dallas Moolteepass is both kickass and vulnerable—a perfect fit for this bipolar film. Bruce Willis nails the role of Korben Dallas, a.k.a.

Future John McClane, Chris Tucker's fast-talking performance as Ruby Rhod pretty much has to be seen to be understood, and Gary Oldman as antagonist Jean-Baptiste Emanuel Zorg may be the most interesting bit about this movie. The twitchy, cruel Zorg is the film's antagonist, and yet at no point in *The Fifth Element*'s entirety do he and Korben Dallas cross paths, or even become *aware* of each other.

Being a child can be an oddly lonely experience. You don't quite understand the world yet, and other kids are frequently bastards. It's no surprise, then, that so many young'uns fantasize about finding that perfect, special friend, which is part of why *E.T. the Extra Terrestrial* appeals to so many people. Based on Steven Spielberg's own childhood experiences with his imaginary friend, *E.T.*'s story is about friendship and that innocent sense of wonder. It's also about a little alien dude. Spielberg is one of the most talented directors to ever come through Hollywood, and it's that ability to draw deep from his own childhood and truly remember what it feels like to be a kid which helped create so many of his classic movies. Both the movie and the alien of the same name have that great, wide-eyed wonderment to them, and they're so heartfelt that audiences everywhere couldn't help but fall in love.

Oh, man, with a property as influential as *Star Wars,* it's tough to know where to begin. Few movies have so globally influenced the shape of film, fiction, and popular culture as much as the *Star Wars* films have. First and foremost, the first *Star Wars* helped bring awareness of science fiction to the general public. Before *Star Wars,*[59] most popular movies leaned toward realism rather than the kind of fantastic worlds, creatures, and situations found in sci-fi. Part of that was due to technological limitations, but it was also because most people either thought of science fiction as cheesy, kid's stuff, or

---

[59] Are there many people who refer to *Star Wars* by its technical name, *A New Hope*? I think most just call it *Star Wars* the same way they might refer to *The Fellowship of the Ring* as *The Lord of the Rings*.

they didn't think of it at all. Sure, *Star Wars* was preceded by some sci-fi classics such as the *Planet of the Apes* series, *2001: A Space Odyssey*, and the Italian film *Scarmiglione and the Sandwich of the Stars*, but those kinds of awesome flicks were few and far between.

Once *Star Wars* hit, it hit *big.* It launched the careers of several of Hollywood's most powerful players, and it fostered the idea of the summer blockbuster. You know those awesome, big-budget flicks that come out during the summer because everyone has the free time to go see them? That didn't really happen before *Star Wars* came along.

Geeky Influences: Star Wars

Star Wars **tattoos.** We geeks dig our tats—a cool symbol or logo provides a great way of immortalizing exactly how important something is to you. While many geeky properties are quite tatt-able,[60] *Star Wars* might be the most highly tatt-ified.[61] The many insignias for the Rebel Alliance, Imperial Army, Mandalorian Bounty Hunters, and, of course, motherflipping Ewoks are emblazoned on the skin of geeks everywhere as a way of proudly proclaiming whether they roll with the light side or party with the dark.

So many catch phrases, gadgets, and characters irrevocably embedded in the public's consciousness. Lightsabers, Darth Vader, Chewbacca the Wookie, Princess Leia's hair, "I know." While any given person may not be able to re-enact *Return of the Jedi* start to finish, there are countless bits of *Star Wars*-y goodness that have become damn near universally known.

For more movies about aliens who are more interested in interpersonal connections than they are in eating our faces off, check out: *Avatar, Enemy Mine, Galaxy Quest, The Last Starfighter, Lilo & Stitch, Alien Nation, The Day the Earth Stood Still, The Iron Giant,* and *Escape to Witch Mountain.*

---

[60] This is a real word.

[61] This is also a real word. Don't look it up, just trust me. Hey, I see that smart phone! Don't you dare Google anything!

Five Things from Star Wars that Could Also Be Euphemisms for Your Genitals

5 | Lightsaber

4 | Death Star

3 | Millennium Falcon

2 | Old Ben Kenobi

1 | Sarlacc Pit

Alien Jerkwads, Douchebags, and Weirdos

Now, just because the last few movies I've discussed are about extraterrestrials being more or less nice doesn't mean you should expect them *all* to be nice. Ever since the first prop guy spray-painted some paper plates silver and put them in front of a camera, people have been obsessed with the dilemma as to whether there's intelligent life out there ... and whether it wants to kill us.

The *Alien* series answers both questions with a resounding *yes*. In space, no one can hear when you throw up because you saw a dude's chest get blown open and a freaky phallic monster came screaming out. *Alien* is the quintessential sci-fi horror flick; thanks to its fantastic direction, casting, and special effects, the film can terrify modern audiences just as well as it did decades ago. Much of *Alien*'s power comes from the actual alien itself. The Xenomorph spends most of the film as a rarely seen foe, slinking around in shadows and only exposing its tail or pinky toe until nearly the end of the film. The truest sort of horror comes from that which we cannot know or

define; Lovecraft built an entire career writing scary stories about horrifying horror so horrific you can't even *comprehend* it (but we'll talk more about H.P. in a bit).

The Thing's[62] horrifying effectiveness hasn't waned with time, either, and like *Alien*, much of that stems from its practical special effects. In both movies, the human protagonists are reacting to very real stimuli. There's no tennis ball on a stick and green screen here; what we see is what they saw. Kurt Russell gives a balls-out awesome performance as the tougher-n-nails MacReady. Few films manage to so quickly, so *succinctly,* summarize a character as *The Thing* does. In R.J. MacReady's first

---

[62] One of my favorite things about John Carpenter's *The Thing* is that it's a story told in three parts. Chronologically, events take place in this order: (1) *The Thing*, a prequel starring Mary Elizabeth Winstead and released in 2011, followed by (2) *The Thing* (John Carpenter's original movie), and then (3) *The Thing*, a video game, which includes characters from the film and counts as canon. Yes, that's right, *The Thing* trilogy consists of *The Thing*, *The Thing*, and *The Thing*.

scene, we see him playing chess against a computer; when it defeats him, he pours his drinks into his circuits and fries the sucker. "Cheatin' bitch," he says as the sparks fly. MacReady's a guy who will win at any cost, even if it means destroying everything, himself included, in the process.

You might categorize *Predator* as a genre-straddling film, because at times it's a traditional action movie, but it's also sci-fi horror, and then it's *also* kind of a western, in that the human characters and the Predator itself operate by their own internal codes of honor. Its story is simple: Arnold Schwarzenegger and his merry band of badasses are on a mission in the jungle, and during their mission, they get stalked and picked off one-by-one by some unseen, otherworldly hunter. Like most good horror movies, this film relies on our imaginations to enhance the terror. It's a *while* before we have any idea what the eponymous Predator looks like, and even longer before we get a peek behind its mask to see what it *really* looks like. Early on in the film, all we get are voyeuristic, first-person shots of its heat vision as it tracks Arnold and his crew. Oh, and the flayed trophies of its victims.

A crapload of people bite the big one in *Predator*, but the members of Arnold's team are all memorable, despite mostly being there to add to the Predator's body count. Jesse "The Body" Ventura throws around insane one-liners like a daily wisdom calendar gone horribly wrong. Carl Weathers brings some humanity, some inter-personal conflict, and some good old Carl Weathers handsomeness to the affairs. There's also a soldier whose name isn't important since most folks just call him Vagina Jokes Guy ... because he mostly goes around making vagina jokes.[63] Okay, so they're not all the deepest of characters, but there's life to them, which makes the action much more

---

[63] Fun fact: The actor who played Vagina Jokes Guy is none other than Shane Black, director of the smash-freaking-hit *Iron Man 3*.

intense when they're facing off against such a brutal (and unrelenting) foe.

For more movies about aliens engaging in various levels of a-hole behavior, check out: *Evolution, Independence Day, Close Encounters of the Third Kind, Fire in the Sky, Battlefield Earth, Invasion of the Body Snatchers, Killer Klowns from Outer Space,*[64] *Attack the Block, Plan 9 From Outer Space,* and *They Live.*

 ## Alternate Names Arnie Suggested For the Movie *Predator*

- Arnold Schwarzenegger Versus Monster Face
- Killer Mans
- Terminator
- Bloodthirsty Death Thing From The Outer Spaces
- Gary

Explorers of the Unknown

Exploration has always been a key element of human culture. Finding new places to live helps manage the population, gather resources, and spread our genes around. Maybe if bees had gotten up off their stingers once in a while and checked out some caves or plains, they might've evolved to be the dominant species. But they didn't, and that's why humanity is #1, baby!

Numerous geeky flicks have tapped into that same longing to wander. *The Adventures of Buckaroo Banzai Across the 8th Dimension* really exemplifies the human spirit's burning desire to explore. In it, Buckaroo Banzai and his Hong Kong Cavaliers are a group of multi-talented geniuses (Buckaroo himself is physicist/neurosurgeon/test pilot, as well as the lead singer of the Hong Kong Cavaliers' band), who end up stumbling across an interdimensional threat after a test run of a new jet engine-powered pickup truck goes awry. Eventually they engage in some soft-spoken heroics with a heavy undercurrent of facetious comedy, and everyone's raw enthusiasm for science, and life in general, infiltrates the film like the finest of ninjas.

For more movies that celebrate science and exploration, check out: *Jurassic Park, Contact, The Abyss, Prometheus,* and any of the *Star Trek* films. Oh, and pretty much anything starring Jeff Goldblum.

---

[64] Is *Killer Klowns from Outer Space* good, in the traditional sense? Hell no. Is it good in the "get a bunch of friends and make fun of this nutso movie?" Hell yes.

Jeff Goldblum

"That is one big pile of shit."

The Man Who Laid the Golden Blum, Jeff Goldblum, brings his trademark wit and intelligence to every role. In *Independence Day*, he played a fast-talking, sexy scientist. In *Jurassic Park*, he played a fast-talking, sexy scientist.[65] In *The Fly*, he played a fast-talking, sexy scientist who becomes decidedly un-sexy after he gets turned into a mutant fly dude. As *Jurassic Park*'s Dr. Ian Malcolm, he's thoughtful, talkative, and not afraid to put the moves on Alan Grant's girlfriend *right in front of him*. He also provides a number of the film's most memorable lines and succinct theses on the dangers of science advancing without proper precautions being taken.

BEEP BOOP: Robots in Film

There are a number of theories regarding exactly how humanity will devise its own demise. Perhaps Country A will get so mad at Country B that they start exchanging nuclear blows, resulting in a *Fallout*-esque post-apocalyptic scenario.

---

[65] Technically he was a Chaotician, but you get my drift.

Maybe, in our attempts to extend life, we will engineer a zombie virus and lead to an undead Armageddon. Or we may simply continue enhancing artificial intelligence technology until it's so advanced it doesn't need us anymore (a point known as the *technological singularity*).

Well, if there's anything to be gleaned from the *Terminator* films, we're definitely headed for Scenario C. The first film blends elements of a horror movie (nigh-unstoppable evil stalks the innocent) with existential crises (what does it mean to be human, are we advancing too quickly without pausing to consider the consequences?) and a little bit of Arnold Schwarzenegger's butt. While this first flick was successful, *Terminator 2: Judgment Day* transformed this unusual sci-fi horror film into one of the most notable science fiction franchises of the last twenty-five years.

James Cameron may not be known for going cheap with his films, but holy bajiminy willikers does he know how to get a good return for his investment. Take, if you will, the curious case of *Terminator 2: Judgment Day*. When it was released in 1991, it was among the priciest flicks ever put to film. "You're crazy!" said some naysayers. "It's too expensive!" cried others. "You've gone maaaad with poooower!" called no-one. Though *T2* had many studio heads worried, once the response from the box office and the critics came in, their worries mysteriously vanished.

It makes sense that *T2* performed so well: it's flipping awesome. It's gritty and grim without getting excessive about it, or lacking a sense of humor. It also features Sarah Connor, one of popular culture's greatest heroines. In the first *Terminator*, Sarah Connor was a mundane, terrified waitress, but in *T2* we have a woman steeled by the deadly truth, dedicating her life to prepare for the inevitable conflict. Her toughness comes with a price, though—she's so ready to fight robots, that she's not so great at connecting with others. Linda Hamilton absolutely kills it as Sarah Connor, balancing her hardness and humanity like a veteran tightrope walker strolling across the big top.[66]

For a man not generally famous for playing deep characters, Arnold Schwarzenegger goes through a hell of an arc as the T-800. He begins the film as a complex, but unerringly straightforward, machine, and ends it as the closest thing to a father John Connor ever had. T-800's nemesis, the T-1000, is as memorable a villain as Sarah Connor is a hero. Robert Patrick conveys a sense of both menace and intellect with a simple *look*. Unlike most of the CGI from the early '90s, the T-1000's liquid metal morphing still holds up today, and much of that is thanks

---

[66] Lena Headey, who followed up Linda Hamilton's triumphant turn as Sarah Connor when she starred in the *Terminator* television series, also shreds the screen with the power of her performance.

Twenty-Five Quotes Only Geeky
Movie Aficionados Will Fully Appreciate

25 | Lower me into the steel. – *Terminator 2: Judgment Day*

24 | Ba weep gra na weep ni ni bong. – *Transformers: The Movie*

23 | I love this plan! I'm excited to be a part of it! – *Ghostbusters*

22 | Do not want. – The bootleg Chinese translation of *Star Wars Episode III: Revenge of the Sith*, titled, *Star War the Third Gather: Backstroke of the West*

21 | This drink—I like it. Another! – *Thor*

20 | Hello. My name is Inigo Montoya. You killed my father. Prepare to die. – *The Princess Bride*

19 | There is no spoon. – *The Matrix*

18 | You're tearing me apart, Lisa! – *The Room*

17 | Klaatu Barada Nikto. – *The Day the Earth Stood Still*

16 | Klaatu Barada ... (*Coughs something unintelligible*). – *Army of Darkness*

15 | Well, double dumbass on you! – *Star Trek IV: The Voyage Home*

14 | Sixty-nine, dude! – *Bill & Ted's Excellent Adventure*

13 | Sorry, Philip. – *Shaun of the Dead*

12 | Nuke the entire site from orbit—it's the only way to be sure. – *Aliens*

11 | All those moments will be lost in time... like tears in rain. – *Blade Runner*

10 | You shall not pass! – *The Lord of the Rings: The Fellowship of the Ring*

9 | Pay no attention to the man behind the curtain! – *The Wizard of Oz*

8 | Flynn! Am I still to create the perfect system? – *Tron: Legacy*

7 | It's a trap! – *Star Wars Episode VI: Return of the Jedi*

6 | "One thing about living in Santa Carla I never could stomach ... all the damn vampires."
– *The Lost Boys*

5 | When this baby hits eighty-eight miles per hour, you're gonna see some serious shit.
– *Back to the Future*

4 | You and your stupid minds. Stupid, stupid! – *Plan 9 From Outer Space*

3 | Oh, a fellow chucker, eh? *badass guitar lick* – *Teenage Mutant Ninja Turtles*

2 | Broke into the wrong goddamn rec room, didn't you, you bastard! – *Tremors*

1 | Zombies, man. They creep me out. – *Land of the Dead*

to the combination of practical effects with smart use of CG. Again, it all comes back to James Cameron knowing how to spend his budget—*Titanic, Avatar,* and *Terminator 2: Judgment Day* all cost a buttload,[67] but ended up making it all back and then some. With major money comes major success.

And, occasionally, major quotability.

I, Robot is another big-budget bohunk that achieved strong theatrical success while maintaining some semblance of philosophical complexity. Sure, this blockbuster may have missed a few of the finer points of Isaac Asimov's original works, but that doesn't mean that it's not fun to watch, nor that the filmmakers didn't *try* to put some thought into things. A major theme within *I, Robot* is the classic sci-fi conundrum as to what, exactly, it is that makes us human, and at what point does Artificial Intelligence just become Intelligence?

" ... Who am I?"

"How did I get here?"

"Why do I love overalls so much?"

These are but a few of the questions that plagued the minds of every man, person, and Urkel in the '90s. It's safe to say that the '90s were an existential decade, and with the invention of the internet, it raised further questions of what it meant to be human: are we merely defined by the meatsuits which contain our minds, or does the idea of "self" extend far beyond our skins and glands? *The Matrix* bullet-timed this heady philosophical idea head-on, mostly through the use of fist-fights, computer-animated choreograph, and a crapload of gunplay. Unlike its two much-maligned sequels, the original *Matrix* is heavy on the bad guy beat downs, light on the philosophy. This was the Wachowski siblings' breakout film—it made Lawrence Fishburne famous for something other than a cowboy named Curtis, and Keanu Reeves famous for being something other than an air guitar-ing time traveler or a dude on a speeding bus. There's also, of course, Hugo Weaving, who traded his suit and earpiece for an Elven tunic when he portrayed Elrond in the *Lord of the*

---

[67] Or, in *Titanic*'s case, a boatload. Wokka wokka!

Rings films—giving him two successful trilogies in just a handful of years! Perhaps only Weaving's *Rings* costar Ian McKellan can boast such an accomplishment.

For more films featuring artificial intelligences who endeavor to be equal to (or greater than) humans, check out: *AI, Bicentennial Man, Short Circuit, Wall-E, Metropolis, Batteries Not Included, Tron, Tron: Legacy,* and, of course, *Blade Runner.*

Geekumentaries

A number of great documentary films highlight people with geeky zeal. *Trekkies* and its follow-up, *Trekkies 2*, are a couple of the more well-known geekumentaries. Both flicks focus on some of *Star Trek*'s most intensely devoted fans, like the woman so wrapped up in *Trek* that she wore her Federation uniform when she was a juror in the Whitewater scandal trial.

If you're interested in LARPing,[68] *Monster Camp* would probably be of interest to you. Running around in black face makeup and leather armor may seem silly to some, but with an enthusiastic group of people, it's a way of breaking out of the ordinary, making friends, and having fun. There are many different types of LARPing, but the gleeful role-players of *Monster Camp* focus on playing NERO, a game with heavy emphasis on fantasy, character interaction, and numbers-based combat with foam weapons and bags of birdseed.

Jiro Dreams of Sushi may not be the first thing that comes to mind if someone mentions geeky documentaries, but it certainly qualifies. In it we learn about Jiro Ono, who is probably history's greatest sushi chef, and the kind of obsessive devotion he puts into his favorite food. On the surface, this flick centers around a dude who can't get enough of that rice-y, seafood-y goodness, but underneath that simple exterior, you'll find a look into the mind of a genius, a true *master* of his craft. You could say that the sort of unyielding diligence Jiro applies to sushi is probably the same as any of history's greatest minds and masters. At 85, Jiro shows no signs of stopping; the day he makes his last sushi will probably be the day he goes to the great sushi bar in the sky. It's tough for any master to realize that he or she will never live forever, and that once they're gone, many of their deepest secrets will be gone with them. Jiro, however, can rest a little easier knowing that, while he's undisputedly the #1 sushi chef in the world, the #2 spot is a tie between his two sons.

---

[68] Live Action Role-Playing.

For more documentaries devoted to geeky cultures and obsessed masters, check out: *American Scream, The Dungeon Masters, Make Believe, Indie Game, King of Kong: A Fistful of Quarters,* and *Buskers.*

Monstrously Mashed Movies

Monster movies have been a staple of American cinema ever since Ray Harryhausen picked up his first wire-framed figure and took pictures of it, frame by painstaking frame. These flicks are often low on plot, high on body counts, and have the sad problem of aging far worse than most other films because of technological progression—it's tough to scare a modern audience with costumes made of Styrofoam and duct tape.

Many mutant mooks have traipsed across cinema screens over the years, eventually giving way to the lower-budget, higher-gore genre of slasher movies, but as the list on pages 110 and 111 shows, there are a few beasts who stand out head, shoulders, and tentacles above the rest.

Super Ghosts and Goblins

Big old monsters aren't the only type of terror to be found in geeky sci-fi flicks. There's also goblins, those nasty little green critters with a frequent hankering for gold, and g-g-g-ghosts!

Few ghost movies can stack up the scares the way *Poltergeist* does. Here you have a haunted house movie done to absolute perfection—nearly every movie involving a bad real estate purchase and a ghost or two has tried to emulate *Poltergeist*, and they usually fail. Like a fine plate of nachos, *Poltergeist* is made from only the best ingredients, with the main meat being the sympathetic family and the titular geists, most of whom are terrifying, tortured visions of the afterlife. And who could forget that weird, eclectic team of paranormal investigators, none of whom more memorable than Zelda Rubinstein as the psychic Tangina Barrons.

Though M. Night Shyamalan's later efforts have varied in quality,[69] he put his best foot forward with *The Sixth Sense*.[70] This supernatural thriller is moody as *balls,* with stellar performances from stars Bruce Willis and Haley Joel Osment. It's a bummer that the world probably won't ever experience a film like *The Sixth Sense* again; at least, not the same way. So much of the film's power centers around its twist ending that today's perpetually online and overly connected world would ruin. All it takes is a lone goober tweeting, "OMG CNAT BLEVE BRUS WILLIS WUZ GHOST ENTIRE TIME #holla" to destroy the whole experience.

While *Poltergeist* and *The Sixth Sense* are tense, often frightening affairs, not every ghost movie has to be. Writer/director/weird-hair-haver Tim Burton seems obsessed with the afterlife and the undead and brought us his spooky, hilariously macabre vision of it with *Beetlejuice*.[71] Way before Timmy B. was directing billion-dollar 3-D

---

[69] I've theorized that M. Night Shyamalan's fame is due to a demonic pact stating that his first movie will be a massive success, and each film after that will be of gradually decreasing quality. Check out his IMDB page and tell me I'm wrong.

[70] Warning: I'm going to spoil the ending to *The Sixth Sense* later. If you haven't seen it already, shame on you, because that movie's like fifteen years old.

[71] Beetlejuice. BEETLEJUICE!

Nine Movie Monsters Who Don't Let Fame Go to Their Heads Regardless of Whether They Have Heads

GODZILLA

Source film: *Godzilla*
Monster type: Giant Lizard
Rivals: Mecha-Godzilla, King Ghidora, Mecha-Ghidora, Gigan, Biollante
Friends: Godzooky/Minilla (son), Captain Carl Majors, Dr. Quinn Darien, Pete, Brock, Anguirus, Gamera, Rodan, Mothra
Powers: Atomic fire breath, nuclear pulse, magnetic aura, eye lasers, rapid regeneration, and generally behaving like a boss

KING KONG

Source film: *King Kong*
Monster type: Giant ape
Friends: Little Kong (son), Lady Kong, Donkey Kong
Rivals: Godzilla, Gorosaurus, Mechani-Kong
Powers: Monkey business

THE THING

Source film: *The Thing*
Nemesis: MacReady
Monster type: Shapeshifter
Powers: Rapid regeneration, cell division, shapeshifting, and looking really, really gross
Weakness: Fire

THE BLOB

Source film: *The Blob*
Monster type: Amorphous blob
Powers: Absorbing living things to increase its mass; generally being ooky
Weakness: Calling it fat

GRABOIDS

Source film: *Tremors*

Nemeses: Burt Gummer, Val and Earl

Monster type: Underground bug-esque things with snake things coming out of their mouth-things

Powers: Rapid subterranean movement, casual evolution into new species depending on whether or not the sequel needs it

Weakness: Lack of traditional vision

MOGWAI

Source film: *Gremlins*

Friends: Billy and that old Asian dude

Monster type: Fuzzy little furballs

Powers: Reproduce when exposed to water; shapeshift into reptilian gremlins if they eat after midnight

THE CLOVERFIELD MONSTER

Source film: *Cloverfield*

Monster type: Big ass bug lizard

Powers: Spawn broodlings, being impervious to shaky-cam induced motion sickness

IT

Source film: *It*

Nemesis: The Losers

Monster type: Shapeshifter

Powers: Taking on the guise of whatever you find scariest, which generally means that It runs around as a friggin' clown

XENOMORPHS

Source film: *Alien*

Nemesis: Ellen Ripley

Monster type: Alien

Rival: Other aliens

Powers: Parasitic infestation, rapid evolution based on its host creature, acid blood, extra tiny little mouths

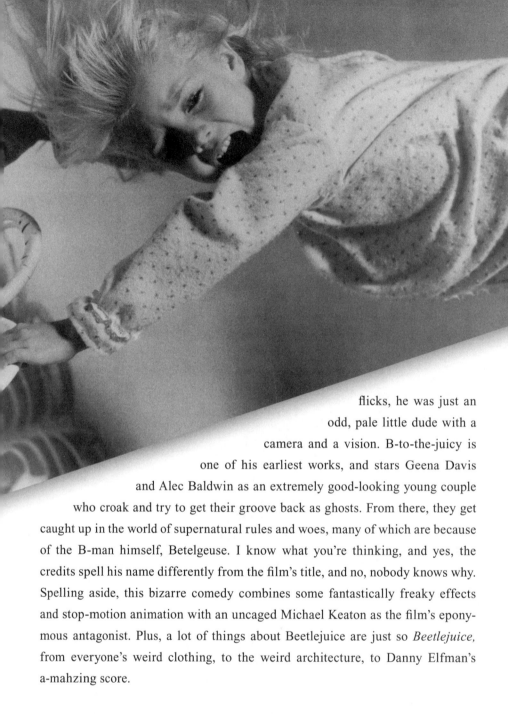

flicks, he was just an odd, pale little dude with a camera and a vision. B-to-the-juicy is one of his earliest works, and stars Geena Davis and Alec Baldwin as an extremely good-looking young couple who croak and try to get their groove back as ghosts. From there, they get caught up in the world of supernatural rules and woes, many of which are because of the B-man himself, Betelgeuse. I know what you're thinking, and yes, the credits spell his name differently from the film's title, and no, nobody knows why. Spelling aside, this bizarre comedy combines some fantastically freaky effects and stop-motion animation with an uncaged Michael Keaton as the film's epony-mous antagonist. Plus, a lot of things about Beetlejuice are just so *Beetlejuice,* from everyone's weird clothing, to the weird architecture, to Danny Elfman's a-mahzing score.

Folks, there are some films you love so freaking much that you don't know where to start—it'd be like trying to explain why water is good, or why you prefer breathing to not breathing. It's a comfort movie that you've probably carried with you all of your life; one that you can watch at any time and know you'll enjoy it. Everyone's got their go-to flick, and for me, it's *Ghostbusters*. I've seen the exploits of the boys in brown so many times I could probably perform *Ghostbusters: A One Man Play* by Alex Langley. There just aren't enough good things I can say about this blisteringly funny, fantastically original movie (though that won't stop me from trying).

Let's start with the actors—every part, big and small, is perfectly cast and performed. Sigourney Weaver brings a wry wit to Dana Barrett, keeping things fun in what might have otherwise been a dull, thankless part. Canadian comedy genius Rick Moranis' performance as Dana's prying neighbor, Louis Tully, provides a constant stream of oddball mannerisms and funny, often improvised lines.[72] Bill Murray's Peter Venkman struts about with an untouchable confidence. Everything he does seems to be for his own (and the audience's) amusement. He's snarky, he's mischievous, he's just a little bit sleazy, and he's absolutely perfect. Winston (Ernie Hudson) helps keep everything in perspective as the "working-man's Ghostbuster." True Believer Akroyd brings an earnestness to his character, Ray Stanz, which nicely counterbalances Peter's sarcasm and Egon's (Harold Ramis) encyclopedic intellect.

The success of *Ghostbusters* lead to *Ghostbusters II*, as well as a mega-successful Saturday morning cartoon. There have also been talks of a *Ghostbusters III* for years, but the script has been caught in development Hell for a long time, which may be for the best given that Akroyd's idea for *Ghostbusters III* was to actually send the Ghostbusters to Hell.

Speaking of movies that will make you laugh, if you're a fan of cheese and you've never seen *Troll 2,* man, start streaming that bad boy right now. I can wait.

... You finished it? Wasn't it *insane?* How about that scene where the goblin queen makes out with the dude by using corn, and then it explodes into popcorn? Or where that one guy goes jogging while drinking a ton of milk, then gets sick from it? Looks like milk was a bad choice.

In case you haven't gathered, *Troll 2* is frigging *nuts.* There's not a troll to be found in it—the movie's antagonists are goblins, but in reality, they're little people wearing cheesy masks and burlap sacks. Nearly everything anyone does is so weird, stilted, and just plain *off* from how real human beings behave. There's also other

---

[72] That speech Louis gives at his party, the one where he talks about Nova Scotian salmon, acetylsalicylic acid, and how he threw the party as a business promotion so he could use it as a tax write-off? Rick Moranis improvised that entire bit. There's a lot of great improv in *Ghostbusters*, but that piece might be the most impressive simply because of how *long* Louis goes on for.

miscellaneous insanity, like the ghost grandpa who can freeze time (which he does to buy his grandson the precious seconds he needs to pee all over everyone's poisoned meal), or resident nerd Arnold's utterly amazing delivery of the line, "They're eating her. And then they're going to eat me. OH MY GOOOOOD!" *Troll 2* is, and I say this unironically, one of the most entertaining things I've ever seen.

If you can't get enough movies featuring ghosts and/or goblins, check out: *The Ring, The Frighteners, Paranormal Activity, Ghost* (The Patrick Swayze movie) *The Grudge, Thirteen Ghosts,*[73] *Spider-Man,* and *The Lord of the Rings* trilogy.

Where We're Going, We Don't Need Roads: Time Travel Movies

While hard science fiction often enjoys dreaming about the mechanics behind speculative science, "soft" science fiction stories generally concern themselves less with the behind-the-scenes stuff and more on using science fiction as a vehicle for character development and storytelling. Who knows whether *Back to the Future*'s science holds up against actual time travel, but it sure is one of the most universally beloved movies to come out in the last several decades.

Marty's personal journey mirrors that weird experience many teens/young adults go through when they learn to not see their parents as these alien *beings,* but instead find ways to relate to them as people. Before his time-traveling adventure, Marty was accustomed to his dad being the brow-beaten loser he knew in his present, but in the past he was a soft-spoken guy with big dreams and a surreptitiously lustful side. His mom may be a miserable, chain-smoking prude as Marty originally knows her, but in the past she was an energetic, *surprisingly* forward young lady.

Many TV shows have had episodes featuring characters stuck in a temporal loop, doomed to repeat the same events over and over again until they figure out what's going wrong and then break out of it.[74] But when people refer to chronological anoma-

---

[73] *Thirteen Ghosts* may not be that great of a movie, but the Black Zodiac of Thirteen Ghosts are all pretty damn cool, and make the film well worth your time.

[74] Hell, the television series *Seven Days* built its entire premise around re-experiencing the same small window of time.

Doc Brown and Marty

Doc: *"Great Scott!"*

Marty: *"This is heavy, Doc!"*

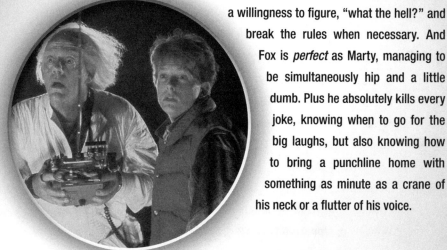

It's hard to find characters and performances as memorable as Christopher Lloyd as Doctor Emmett Brown and Michael J. Fox as Marty McFly. There's such *life* to each of them. Doc has so many great catch phrases, a tendency to spew scientific jargon at a moment's notice, and a willingness to figure, "what the hell?" and break the rules when necessary. And Fox is *perfect* as Marty, managing to be simultaneously hip and a little dumb. Plus he absolutely kills every joke, knowing when to go for the big laughs, but also knowing how to bring a punchline home with something as minute as a crane of his neck or a flutter of his voice.

lies of that nature, what do they call them? A *Groundhog Day.*

That's because (1) *Groundhog Day* is one of the earliest, and most prominent, stories featuring this temporal plot hook, and (2) *Groundhog Day* is awesome. Bill Murray's character, Phil,[75] never finds out *why* he's stuck reliving Groundhog Day

---

[75] Yes, like the groundhog.

over and over. However, after fighting the universe for countless repeated days, he learns to embrace infinity and becomes not only quite adept at several hobbies, but a better person in general. *Groundhog Day* definitely falls on the side of soft sci-fi/fantasy, but its deft blend of comedy and humanity makes it a worthwhile watch for even the most hardcore of geeks.

If you dig time travel movies and want to get caught in a temporal loop so you can experience them again and again, check out: *Déjà Vu, Time Bandits, Timecop, Bill and Ted's Excellent Adventure, The Girl Who Leapt Through Time,* and *Looper.*

 A Few TV Shows with *Groundhog Day* Episodes

- "Cause and Effect" - *Star Trek: The Next Generation*
- "Life Serial" - *Buffy the Vampire Slayer*
- "Mystery Spot" - *Supernatural*
- "Monday" - *The X-Files*
- "I Do Over" - *Eureka*
- "Been There, Done That" - *Xena: Warrior Princess*
- "Back and Back and Back to the Future" - *Farscape*
- "Window of Opportunity" - *Stargate: SG-1*

Fantastical Flicks

Fantasy movies are great for the same reasons that fantasy shows/books are great: you can do whatever you want in them and the audience will be behind it so long as you have some kind of internal logic to it. Does it make scientific sense that

Gandalf can fight a dude made of fire in *The Lord of the Rings*, or that cursed coins will turn you into a skeleton in *The Pirates of the Caribbean*? Hell no! But it makes sense within the movie, and that's all we need.

Hook is the *Wicked* of its day, taking a time-proven story and telling a brand new tale with it. The movie feels as if it's right out of a storybook, from London's frost-bitten streets to the hustle and bustle of the pirates' cove and the Lost Boys splendid and, like, totally organic hideout. The strong cast helps this movie stay good after repeated viewings, like Dante Basco as Rufio, the obnoxious, hot-headed, and kind of awe-some new leader of the Lost Boys. There's also forty-year-old Robin Williams giving a transforma-tive performance; Peter Panning's the worst kind of modern man— a guy who has no idea how boring he is and how he's spending his energy in all the wrong places. Later we get Williams as a newly Peter Pan-fied guy, bounding around like a kid a quarter his age. Few on-screen duos provide as much goofy fun as the dynamic between Dustin Hoffman as Captain Hook and Bob Hoskins as his right hand man, Smee. Captain Hook is a real actor's villain. The guy's well-read, contemplative, and has a heart as black as coal all the way to the end. Smee, on the other hand, isn't so much a *bad* guy as he is a guy who knows how to get along.

Dance, magic dance! Jump, magic jump! Labyrinth may be more of a cult classic than a widespread hit, but even today you can still see the impact of this wildly imaginative film. Jim Henson Company went all-out with this richly imaginative flick, filling with the best damn puppet work around, an original and interesting world, and a soundtrack so maddeningly catchy, it'll infect your brain and stick with you for the rest of your life (its songs can be *so cruel)*. And then there's David Bowie as the Goblin King. He's a nuanced guy, to be sure. He's fond of deception and misdirection, and doesn't mind being rotten once in a while, but beneath it all he's just a lonely dude tired of being surrounded by those cackling idiot goblins all day long.

For more films which delve into the fantastic, check out: *The Lord of the Rings* trilogy, the *Hobbit* trilogy, all ninety-seven *Harry Potter* movies, *The Pirates of the Caribbean,*[76] *The Princess Bride, Hellboy, Jason and the Argonauts,* and Studio Ghibli's *Spirited Away.*

GEEK Spotlight

Hayao Miyazaki

"Life is a winking light in the darkness."

Miyazaki has often been called the Japanese Walt Disney—the man's contributions to animation are prolific, to say the least. Dozens of films and short films have been made under the banner of his animation company, Studio Ghibli, and while most are friendly, all-aged affairs, they also offer far more moral complexity than you'll usually find in the cinema. Miyazaki's films tend to lack traditional antagonists, and when there is a villain, their villainy tends not to be so clear-cut— more often they're not bad, they're just misguided. Miyazaki's films are filled to the brim with magic, wonderment, and awesome animation, and they also tend to feature strong female protagonists.

---

[76] You really only need to check the first one. Your mileage may vary on the other three.

If you love that anime look and want to catch more movies with that fine anime flavor, check out: the aforementioned *Spirited Away, The Girl Who Leapt Through Time, Akira, Howl's Moving Castle, Princess Mononoke, My Neighbor Totoro, Ponyo, Grave of the Fireflies,*[77] *Ghost in the Shell, The Cat Returns, Cowboy Bebop: The Movie,*[78] *and Redline.*

Those Zany Zombies

It's not clear exactly what incited it, but lately it seems as if there are zombies *everywhere.* Zombie movies, zombie versions of all of your favorite characters, zombies on your lawn, etc. While the rules may change slightly depending on the story, in general, there are a few universal truths to the walking dead:

1. They have an unending hunger for the flesh of the living.
2. Their bites are fatal.
3. A shot to the head keeps them dead.

Bela Lugosi's *White Zombie* may be the first "zombie" movie, but since it makes use of the z-word to mean "voodoo slave" rather than "animated, cannibalistic corpse," it's not really what most think of as when they hear the word zombie. It wasn't until George Romero's *Night of the Living Dead* did we see the undead hordes we've come to know and fear.[79] Romero drew influence from Richard Matheson's classic novella *I Am Legend* in creating *Night of the Living Dead.* It's the tale of a group of survivors banding together to make it through the night in a world riddled with zombies—a formula that virtually all later zombie films copied. Sometimes the plot varies as to whether the survivors are trying to survive where they are, escape their location, or (occasionally) cure the undead plague. Interestingly enough, while nearly every other zombie film is content to ape Romero's basic formula, he was not, and set out to do something different with each of his subsequent films.

Dawn of the Dead used zombies as a metaphor for the mall-obsessed consumerism that wracked American culture in the late 1970s and 1980s. *Day of the Dead* explored how the lack of inter-human communication could lead to unrest and chaos. *Land of the Dead* drew from themes of class warfare, as well as providing commentary on the United States' involvement in Iraq. *Diary of the Dead* was told in a "found footage"

---

[77] Although save this one for when you're in the mood to bawl your eyes out.
[78] Otherwise known as *Cowboy Bebop: Knocking On Heaven's Door.*
[79] It was also one of the first films to feature an African-American lead, which, in 1968, was a controversial move. Romero's reasoning behind his casting of Duane Jones as hero Ben? Jones "simply gave the best audition."

EN THERE'S NO MORE ROOM IN HELL... THE DEAD WILL WALK THE EARTH!

format, a format which Romero thought was going to be a groundbreaking move in horror ... until some goober named J.J. Abrams had the same idea and made *Cloverfield*.[80] *Survival of the Dead* looked at xenophobia, and the destruction brought on by lingering resentment.

While a bulk of the work behind the original *Night of the Living Dead* was performed by George Romero, his filmmaking partner, John Russo, did help him create the movie, and, after a bit of squabbling, the two of them split ways, with Romero taking the "of the Dead" name for himself, and Russo taking "of the Living Dead." Russo would later go on to create the *Return of the Living Dead* series. While these flicks are a bit on the brainless side, they're also, ironically, the source of the cry of "Brains!" often attributed to zombies.

There are *tons* of zombie movies out there, and most of them are giant piles of crap. If you're lucky, they're so bad they're good for a laugh, like *The Dead Hate the Living,* with its strange brand of over-acting, terrible special effects, and theme song by the hilariously named Penis Flytrap. *Children of the Living Dead* is another flick chock full of continuity errors and general stupidity, which may be surprising considering that it opens with a pretty badass sequence of Tom Savini taking down a zombie horde and rescuing some kids. Unfortunately, more zombie movies are closer to *Zombie Apocalypse* in quality and suck vigorously, or are painfully unfunny attempts to subvert the genre, like *Zombies! Zombies! Zombies!* and *Zombie Strippers.*

There have been a few movies that manage to cleverly subvert the tropes and traps common to zombie movies. *Shaun of the Dead* blends the romantic-comedy with

---

[80] And then from there dozens of filmmakers churned out sub-par horror movies, eschewing basic rules of filmmaking in favor of the "found footage" style's cheapness.

Nine Geeky Characters Who, When You Think About It, Could Probably Use a Bath

9 | Pretty much everyone on *The Walking Dead*

8 | Katniss Everdeen

7 | Conan the Barbarian

6 | The Teenage Mutant Ninja Turtles

5 | Blanka

4 | Mad Max

3 | All non-elves in *The Lord of the Rings*

2 | Donkey Kong

1 | Ed from *Shaun of the Dead*

zombie-horror to create the first (and only known) romzomcom. In *Shaun of the Dead*, our titular hero has just been dumped by his girlfriend, the lovely Liz, because he can't sort his freaking life out. He and his best bud Ed try to sort through the wreckage of Shaun's life and future, but before they manage to do anything other than get butt-faced drunk and blare Electro music, zombies invade and ruin everyone's party.

Writer/star Simon Pegg and his frequent collaborator, director Edgar Wright, are lifelong fans of the Zed-word genre. In fact, if you check out *Spaced*, a television show created and written by Pegg, Wright, and Jessica Hynes, you'll see that the episode "Art" is filled with some subtle nods to classic zombie moments (and some

not-so-subtle nods when Simon Pegg's character starts hallucinating that there are undead all around him). *Spaced* is good for more than zombie references, though. It's a fast-paced comedy exploding with love for all things geeky. The cast is great, and Wright directs each episode with the kind of aggressively kinetic energy he's become famous for.

Juan of the Dead brings audiences another clever subversion of the zombie formula. After an undead plague breaks out in Cuba, Juan decides to make a stand on his native soil and open up a business where he and his friends kill your undead loved ones. Though the finale borrows from the traditional dead-head trope of having the characters fight to escape the undead apocalypse, at heart, *Juan of the Dead* is a comedy about national pride.

And then there's *Zombieland*. While the webseries of the same name never gained much traction, this cult classic movie made smart use of its incredible cast to create another great zombie comedy. There are a lot of memorable moments throughout this flick, but the thing most seem to take away from it are its stylish way of espousing the "rules" for a zombie apocalypse. Rules such as: Cardio, The Double Tap, and Enjoy the Little Things. Overall, it's a smartly crafted film made by people who have clearly seen enough zombie movies to know what they should never do or say during a zombie outbreak.

▶ Things You Should Never, Ever Do or Say During a Zombie Outbreak

- Give a snarky speech with your back to a door, wall, or window.
- "I'm going outside to check the fuse box. What? Nah, I don't want anyone to come with me, I'll be fine."
- (When exploring a seemingly empty building) "What do you think is behind *this* door?"
- Try to make sweet love to a zombie because you saw/read *Warm Bodies* and think it might revive them.
- Ask a wild-eyed, pale fellow if he's feeling okay.
- Opt for a convertible because it's "a total babe magnet."
- Give mouth-to-mouth to a passed-out stranger.
- Not take the extra effort to make sure the undead thing you're fighting is *actually* dead.
- Take a bubble bath, alone, and in an abandoned house.
- Ignore bodies you find "just lying around."
- Smoke cigarettes. Zombies or not, they're really bad for you.

First-Hand Geekiness: Zombies

"A lot of writers ascribe the current popularity of zombies to some socio-political angst about the economy and terrorism—zombies as metaphor for the fears and anxieties of a society making commentary on itself. Personally, I tend to think their status as pop culture darlings has more to do with how zombies have been taken out of their proverbial archetypal box. No longer are they merely the mindless, shambling ghouls that we've known and loved for more than forty years. Now they're faster. Funnier. Sentient. They fight for civil rights, are domesticated as house pets, and fall in love. In short, they've become more versatile. More well-rounded. And who doesn't love a well-rounded zombie? Plus they're tragically comical, shuffling along, losing their hair and teeth and the occasional appendage. Add the fact that they used to be us and you can't help but relate, which, ultimately, is why I think we find them so compelling.

I've been a fan of zombies ever since I saw Romero's original *Night of the Living Dead* when I was eleven. While I enjoy other classic monsters, they don't hold quite the same appeal. Maybe that's because I think of them in terms of who I'd want

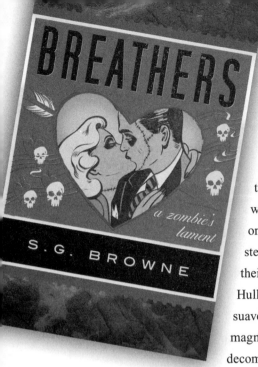

to hang out with. Werewolves are like the jocks of the monster world, full of testosterone and sprouting hair all over the place, channeling their aggression and rage. Meanwhile, vampires are like fraternity boys—all pretty and full of themselves, constantly trying to seduce you with a smokescreen of insincerity. Zombies, on the other hand, are the geeks of the monster world. They don't try to impress you with their charms or their ability to go Incredible Hulk every four weeks. They don't have the suave moves of a vampire or the raw animal magnetism of a werewolf. They wear their decomposing hearts on their sleeves and aren't ashamed to say, "I'm a zombie and I want to eat your brains." They have an unpretentious honesty, which is something you have to admire in a monster."

-S.G. Browne

Author of *Breathers: A Zombie's Lament* and *Fated*

For more movies about zombies, or about creatures who may not *technically* be zombies, but they behave in basically the same way so I'm going to include them anyway, check out: *Night of the Comet, Fido, Warm Bodies, Dance of the Dead, The Signal, Wasting Away, I Am Legend, The Omega Man, The Last Man on Earth, 28 Days Later, 28 Weeks Later, The Re-Animator, Bride of the Re-Animator,* the *Resident Evil* series, the *REC* series (particularly the awesomely nutso *REC 3: Genesis*) and its American counterpart, *Quarantine,* the surprisingly good *Flight of the Living Dead: Outbreak on a Plane,* and, for those who are strong of stomach, Peter Jackson's deranged *Braindead,* also known as *Dead Alive,* also known as *Dear God Why Did You Pick This You're A Sick Bastard, Roger.*

The movies I've listed are among the best the geek world has to offer; the cream of the crop, the pick of the litter, the Gornest of the Gorns. But know that there's a Yin and Yang to geek films. For all the good movies in the world, there must be bad ones.

While most terrible movies at least have their somewhat originality going for them, there are those creepy, crawly things that skitter away at the edge of your sight, the things that geeks everywhere recoil in anger when they hear them spoken of. Brace yourself, because I'm talking about awful remakes and reboots. Or what may be even worse than a terrible reboot is when there's a movie that *shouldn't* have been bad, but, through executive meddling, miscasting, or behind-the-scenes incompetency, they ended up as big fat piles of disappointment.

Ten of the Geek Movie World's Biggest, Fattest Piles of Disappointment

10 | *Dungeons and Dragons*

9 | *John Carter*

8 | *Speed Racer*

7 | *Prometheus*[81]

6 | *Eragon*

5 | *Terminator 3: Rise of the Machines*

4 | *The Last Airbender*

3 | This space reserved for the god-awful Michael Bay *Ninja Turtles* movie, which has yet to come to pass and, if my time machine works, will *never* come to pass.

2 | *Green Lantern*[82]

1 | The *Star Wars* Prequels

---

[81] This one depends on who you ask. I, personally, just *love* movies with vomit-inducing impromptu caesarean section sequences featuring massive internal parasites.

[82] Mini-rant time: I think Ryan Reynolds would have made such a great Wally West Flash. Fast-talking and quippy is right up his alley. Hotshot Hal Jordan? Not so much. Mini-rant complete.

Twelve of the Worst and Most Needless Movie Remakes and Reboots[83]

(12) | **Reboot/Remake:** *Evil Dead* (2013)

What it's a reboot/remake of: *The Evil Dead* (1981), starring Bruce "Don't Call Me Ash" Campbell. While this flick's definitely the best of this bunch, it's still utterly needless. *Cabin in the Woods* utterly, *brilliantly* dissected the laziness of most modern horror films, and how slavishly they adhere to their formulas. So what do we get with the new *Evil Dead*? A movie about five young people getting slaughtered in the woods. Gee, where have we seen this before? Oh yeah, *in the original Evil Dead*.

(11) | **Reboot/Remake:** *Nightmare on Elm Street* (2010)

What it's a reboot/remake of: *Nightmare on Elm Street* (1984)

Jackie Earl Haley was a great choice to play a new, extra-creepy Freddy Krueger, but this unenthusiastic remake ain't got the heft the original does. Plus, why would you recast such an iconic role when your lead, Robert Englund, is still young enough to throw on a hat and razor glove?

(10) | **Reboot/Remake:** *The Invasion* (2007)

What it's a reboot/remake of: *Invasion of the Body Snatchers* (1956)

The Invasion took the paranoid Cold War vibe of the original and sterilized it into something cold and emotionless ... maybe it's some kind of a meta-commentary on remakes in general? Perhaps the director is secretly telling us that this remake is the pod-people version of the original?

(9) | **Reboot/Remake:** *Clash of the Titans* (2010)

What it's a reboot/remake of: *Clash of the Titans* (1981)

How is it that, out of nowhere, Sam Worthington started popping up in such high-investment, high-profile movies? Casting him as a machine in *Terminator 4* made sense, since he acts like one, but why *Clash of the Titans*? Why'd this even need to be *remade*, anyway? Why, I ask you!

(8) | **Reboot/Remake:** *The Day the Earth Stood Still* (2008)

What it's a reboot/remake of: *The Day the Earth Stood Still* (1951)

I'd rather watch *Speed 3: Speed on Ice* than watch Keanu Reeves sleepwalk his way through this one.

(7) | **Reboot/Remake:** *Planet of the Apes* (2001)

What it's a reboot/remake of: *Planet of the Apes* (1968).

---

[83] Special shout-out goes to the failed pilot for the American remake of *The IT Crowd*. It's amazing how flat and utterly unfunny the show is, when it's using almost the same script as the original pilot, word for word, stars snarktastic funnyman Joel McHale as the lead, and even has Richard Ayoade playing Moss again, but doing a worse job! Clearly the people behind the scenes have no idea what they're doing when they make Joel McHale unfunny and get Richard Ayoade to deliver the same lines, only crappier.

Usually, having Mark Wahlberg involved with anything is a bad sign, and Tim Burton kind of went wild with his Burton-y-ness in this one, but not in a good way.

6 | **Reboot/Remake:** *Halloween* (2007)
What it's a reboot/remake of: *Halloween* (1978)
Adding back story to serial killer Michael Myers misses the point— that he was always just supposed to be a purely evil killing machine.

5 | **Reboot/Remake:** *The Stepford Wives* (2004)
What it's a reboot/remake of: *The Stepford Wives* (1975)
This new version can't decide if it's a straight horror movie or a Tim Burton-esque horror comedy, so it plays it safe and ends up in the crappy, passionless middle.

4 | **Reboot/Remake:** *The Omen* (2006)
What it's a reboot/remake of: *The Omen* (1976)
This remake is more soulless than Damien himself.

3 | **Reboot/Remake:** *Bewitched* (2005)
What it's a reboot/remake of: *Bewitched* (1964)
Hmm ... three films on this list starring Nicole Kidman. I'm sensing a pattern, here.

2 | **Reboot/Remake:** *Godzilla* (1998)
What it's a reboot/remake of: *Godzilla* (1954).
Fun fact: in *Godzilla: Final Wars,* we see Big G throw down against pretty much every foe he's ever faced, with a few bonus fights just for fans ... like the giant lizard named "Zilla" who resembles the CG monstrosity from the Emmerich/Devlin movie. Original Godzilla easily trumps Zilla, effortlessly slaying it in under a minute.

1 | **Reboot/Remake:** *Psycho* (1998)
What it's a reboot/remake of: *Psycho* (1960)
When you have a movie so perfect as the original *Psycho,* the only place to go with a remake is down, *especially* when the remake is almost a *shot-for-shot* redo of the original.

Chapter 4

Video Games:

Choosing Your Own Adventure

Most mediums of entertainment, such as movies, television shows, and messages shaved onto the back of dudes' heads, are a one-way experience. They've (hopefully) got something interesting to say and an interesting way of saying it. Video games, however, do the same thing while simultaneously allowing the player to use it as a means of expressing themselves. Sure, player influence is obvious in choice-based titles like any of the post-apocalyptic *Fallout* series or Bioware's science fiction RPG series, *Mass Effect,* but choice factors into other games as well. Would you prefer your character have blonde hair or brown? Do you favor hand-to-hand combat or ranged attacks? Would you rather stick with the burning offensive power of the fire flower, or go for mobility with the cape feather? Video games are similar to paintings, but only if you could both paint on the canvas and the canvas could paint back; they're a two-way avenue of entertainment, one whose richness has only begun to develop.

If You Build It, They May or May Not Come, Depending on, Like, If They're Busy or Whatever

In 1989, game designer/genius/all around pretty sweet dude Will Wright had a simple vision: give players control over a city and the ability to rule it as they saw fit. *SimCity* set a new precedent in gaming; it was both involved and accessible, as well as being highly replayable and nigh-infinitely variable. Benevolent mayors could help their cities thrive and grow into the star-studded metropolises of their dreams. The more devious-minded mayors found delight in sending taxes through the roof, choking the city with pollution and crime, and then, when everything was at its worst, summoning a slew of natural (and unnatural) disasters to level the joint.

Wright captured lightning in a pokeball with *SimCity*, and over the course of the next ten years, he and his companions at Maxis would do it again with several other simulation games: *SimEarth, SimAnt, SimLife, SimCity 2000, SimPart-Time Periodontal Assistant Who Also Moonlights as a Tattoo Artist,* and, of course, *The Sims.* While *SimCity* is all about macro-management—making decisions that will affect your city on a massive scale—*The Sims* is about micro-management. In it, you manage the virtual lives of a handful of virtual people you've customized and created from the ground up. Like *SimCity*, it brought out both the good and evil in players. Kind-hearted players might stick to helping their sims find love, success, and self-improvement. Evil players (a.k.a. everyone) could force their sims to live in filth, drown them, burn them in a house fire, starve them, and, after death's kindly hand takes them away from this life of suffering, *revive* them as twisted, undead reflections of their living selves. Why would people be so cruel to them? Because it's fun, and they're not real.

The Sims is (theoretically) about making your characters happy, as well as, on a baser level, helping them survive. Survival is a key element to the distant cousin of the Sim games: *Minecraft.* Players will find comparable freedom in *Minecraft* as they will in any of the *Sims* titles, but the true joy of playing it comes from two main sources. First, there's the thrill of exploration. You'll plumb dank caves and catacombs, mining for treasure and praying that the things which lurk in the dark don't catch you with an arm full of goodies. You'll spend much of your time treasure hunting, but you'll probably spend even more building things. Want a giant, skull-shaped fortress with hot lava flowing from the eye sockets? Get the materials and build it. Do you dig riding rollercoasters underwater? Who doesn't? Or maybe you're just really hungry and wish you had a giant hot dog. Build that bad boy! You won't be able to eat it, but you *can* act out that childhood dream and live in it.

Eleven of the Greatest Experiences You Can Have While Playing a Video Game

11 | Finishing your first fortress in *Minecraft*.

10 | Getting through *Contra* without using the Konami code.

9 | Finally memorizing the pattern of those damn vanishing blocks in a *Mega Man* game.

8 | Scoring that first sweet piece of epic loot in any MMO.

7 | Getting everyone through *Mass Effect 2's* suicide mission alive.

6 | Curb stomping some locust scum in *Gears of War*.

5 | Coming up against a shotgun spamming/sniper camping/noob tube abusing wang online and then piledriving him/her into the bottom of the scoreboard.

4 | Finishing a *Mario Kart* race in first ... and *then* seeing a blue shell hit you after it doesn't matter anymore.[84]

3 | Surviving the onslaught that is *Dark Souls*.

2 | The first time you *fus-roh-dah* a bear off of a mountain in *The Elder Scrolls V: Skyrim*.

1 | Learning to fly in *Super Mario 64*.

What is perhaps indie gaming's biggest success, *Minecraft* originally began as the brainchild of Swedish programmer Marcus "Notch" Persson, and, thanks to the game's universal appeal, it's available damn near everywhere. You can play *Minecraft* on your phone, *Minecraft* in French, and *Minecraft* with your gophers. Between the childlike wonder of exploration and the ability to build nearly anything, there's something for everyone here.

---

[84] Or conversely, being in second place and popping the bastard in first with a shell right before he/she crosses the finish line, then taking first place for yourself.

Terraria and its sci-fi spiritual successor, *Starbound*, build on much of what makes *Minecraft* great, but with a Metroidvania[85] flair. You can build lava-barfing fortresses, but you're probably going to focus on exploring and hunting around for the next bit of amazing treasure to enhance your character with. The 16-bit art style is a retro bonus for any gamers old enough to remember the days of video game cartridges, but, most importantly, these two games are just friggin' fun.

Dwarf Fortress, while not exactly the most accessible of games, provides unparalleled freedom for players hungry to micro/macro manage a group of dwarves. You'll ensure their survival, help them scour the earth for treasure, and make sure they don't get eaten by a Cthulhu-esque terror from beneath the deep. Mark my words, though: *Dwarf Fortress'* learning curve is *steep,* so steep, you'll probably spend your first few outings tumbling headlong down a hill made of starved dead dwarves. Once you get the hang of it, however, you can do nearly anything your heart desires—harvest and maintain acres of crops, train donkeys to headbutt their opponents to death, incite jealousy in your Dwarven ranks, and more! Other games, such as *Towns* and *Gnomoria,* have built upon the *Dwarf Fortress* formula, trying to decrease the learning curve while also keeping the spirit of nihilistic determination alive.

But it's not all poots and giggles with video games. Some titles are insidious; they're built for fun, sure, but it's a kind of fun that comes with an emotional cost. While some will grab the heartstrings and give them a good tug, others might snip them one at a time until you can't take it anymore. Worst yet are the ones that put the burden of decision-making on you, the player. Games such as these are where the medium excels; they make

---

[85] Metroidvania: a style of game wherein player progression is tied to exploration of the game world and acquisition of new abilities. The genre was popularized by both the Metroid and the Castlevania series. If one were to relate the Metroidvania genre to real life, it's as if your high school graduation ceremony was being held on the roof, and the only way to get there is if you first find a grappling hook gun, then use it to rappel up the side of the building. No grappling hook? You're staying in high school forever.

Tali'Zorah nar Rayya

"And I thought I had a good poker face ..."

Though Tali fans can be a bit weird about their beloved Quarian engineer[86], that doesn't change the fact that she's a hell of a character. Tali's people are akin to space Mormons, leaving their comfortable little homes on pilgrimages for the betterment of their entire culture despite how dangerous it is—their immune systems are wonky, and because of that, they have to live in protective bodysuits. While Tali's all about some cultural betterment, she's also *way* into engineering, and kicking ass alongside Commander Shepard. At the beginning of *Mass Effect*, Tali's a bit sheltered, though she's hardly naive, and feels most comfortable around machines (because she tends to chatter on like a goober when she's nervous). By *Mass Effect 3*'s end (if Tali's still alive), she'll have grown into a confident woman, ready to take on any *bosh'tet* who gets in her way.

you go through an emotional journey, and as you do, you're helping shape the course of your own experience.

For games that require some tough decisions of the player, check out: Telltale Games' *The Walking Dead*, *Heavy Rain*, *Bastion*, the *Dragon Age* series, *Knights of the Old Republic*, and the *Mass Effect* series.

---

[86] "Talimancers," as they're often called, romance Tali in-game and occasionally write possessive fan fiction about her, some going so far as to wonder what this exosuit-clad lady's sweat would smell like and espousing theories based on its likely chemical composition.

Legendary Games: The Best of the Best of the Best of the Best

Art historians often sit around discussing their favorite artists, trying to get inside the heads of the great masters and learning from their genius. How did da Vinci manage to create so much? Why was Seurat so obsessed with tiny friggin' dots? Why does that street caricaturist insist on only doing nude portraits of Uncle Joey from *Full House*? Video game historians do the same thing, but with an extra objective in mind. Not only do they work toward figuring out how the greatest games are put together, they must also endeavor to know the effect it will have on the player (and vice-versa). Will players laugh? Cry? Vommorhea?[87] Let's examine some of the best video games history has to offer, so we can figure out where they went so very *right*.

Few gaming heroes are so well-known and iconic as the boy in blue (and red), Mario. Thanks to the *Mario* games' ease of accessibility and high fun factor, nearly everyone has played as Mario at some point. *Super Mario Bros.* came packaged with every Nintendo Entertainment System, and gamers of every creed, Assassin or otherwise, huddled around the glow of their televisions to aid Mario in his quest to rescue the princess ... a quest that repeatedly confronted players with that maddening phrase: your princess is in another castle.

Its follow-up, *Super Mario Bros. 2*, is the flying sheep of the NES Mario family. The power-ups, enemies, and locales are different from the rest of the titles on Mario's resume, but *SMB2* still has that sense of beguiling oddness you'll find in the other *Mario* titles. Plus you can also play as Luigi and Princess Peach,[88] which is awesome, and Toad, which is less awesome, but still nice. *SMB2* also features Birdo, who was one of, if not *the* first LGBT characters in a video game (in addition to being one goob-tastic looking creature).

Super Mario Bros. 3 should be looked to as a textbook example of how to do a sequel—it gives you everything that's great about the original, but kicked up about a billion notches. Its 8-bit art is expressive, the action is nicely paced, and the game is so over-flowing with hidden areas and secret power-ups that if you added one more, it'd probably burst like a Tanooki-filled dam. The nine worlds of *Super Mario Bros. 3* have a bright, memorable variety to them, covering the kinds of natural environments we all see in our day-to-day lives. You know, stuff such as the arctic, the desert, and freaky carnivorous plant-filled

---

[87] Vommorhea: in medical terms, it's when both ends of your body start pouring out the contents of your stomach like some kind of maniacal faucet.

[88] Or Princess Toadstool, as she was known in those days.

pipe-world. All in all, *Super Mario Bros. 3* is so fun that even the most attention-deficient, Twitter-addicted millennial child can grab a controller and have a good time.[89]

Geeky Influences: *Super Mario Bros.*

Mario helps bridge the gap between all peoples. Everyone—young and old, gamer and non-gamer, Klingon and Romulan—understands Mario. He's one of the most recognizable icons in the world, and his games have an ease of play to them that others *wish* they had.

Mario made overalls and plumbing cool. Okay, not really, but they're a *little* cooler than they used to be.[90]

---

[89] There's so damn many amazing Mario games that it's physically painful for me not to try to mention them all: *Super Mario World, Super Mario 64, Super Mario Galaxy, Mario & Luigi: Superstar Saga, Luigi's Mansion, Luigi's Mansion: Dark Moon*, the *Mario Kart* series, *New Super Mario Bros.*, and the often random, occasionally cruel, frequently hilarious *Mario Party* series.

[90] Although overalls aren't as cool as they were in the '90s, and probably never will be again. The '90s were a simpler, neon-filled time.

If you're looking for a huge fantasy world to explore and set right, look no further than *The Legend of Zelda* series. Each of the many iterations in the *Zelda* games arrive bearing secrets small and large, and don't come into the game expecting it to hold your hand and point you to where every little bit of treasure is—much like being a real explorer, half the fun is finding that there's something out there, regardless of what that something is. The original *Legend of Zelda* was born from series creator and Nintendo god Shigeru Miyamoto's childhood memories of being lost in the countryside without a map to guide him. According to Miyamoto, he "went hiking and found a lake. It was quite a surprise for me to stumble upon it. When I traveled around the country without a map, trying to find my way, stumbling on amazing things as I went, I realized how it felt to go on an adventure like this."

The *Zelda* franchise has over a dozen entries (and counting), but few have the nigh-universal acclaim of the SNES classic *The Legend of Zelda: A Link to the Past*. Not only did *Link to the Past* sharpen the series' trademark dungeon-exploring, artifact-hunting formula, it was also the first game to utilize Nintendo's favorite trick in its arsenal: The Dark World. Nowadays, the existence of *Link to the Past*'s bizarre Dark World would have probably been spoiled by pre-launch trailers and images. Back in the '90s, however, discovering this entirely new dimension was a mind-blowing event.

The first *Mega Man* may have introduced us to the platform hopping, weapon stealing, Dr. Wily-fighting blue bomber, but *Mega Man 2* took him to new heights, with better bosses, better music, and better, well, everything. It also gave players one of the most awesomely overpowered armaments to ever grace a video game—the Metal Blades. Metal Man's signature attack is an eight-directional, rapid-fire attack that, once acquired, costs Mega Man virtually no weapon energy, and the attack itself is so stupid strong that pretty much every boss crumbles against it, Metal Man included.

Mega Man 2 Protip:

Is it still moving?

- If yes, Metal Blade that sucka!
- If no, find something that's moving, and then Metal Blade that sucka!

Several sequels followed *Mega Man 2*, such as the surprisingly named *Mega Man 3, 4, 5,* and *6,* all for the NES. *Mega Man 7* and *8* came out on the Super Nintendo and Sony Playstation, respectively, and while they were relatively well received, many fans thought they lacked the snap and pizzazz of early *Mega Man* titles.[91] This inspired Capcom to take the franchise in a new direction with a spin-off. This new *Mega Man* would have sharper graphics, faster gameplay, and a story more complex than "Dr. Wily doing bad things." Thusly, *Mega Man X* was born. Not only does *MMX* build on the *Mega Man* series' formula of "fight eight bosses and take their powers; each boss is weak against the weapon of another," it included a bevy of secrets and power-ups, including a hadoukin' rad *Street Fighter*-inspired unlockable attack. Levels would also change depending on which order you beat them in. Take down Launch Octopus and Sting Chameleon's stage will fill up with water; crush Chill Penguin and Flame Mammoth's lava-laden level will freeze up like a popsicle. As the *Mega Man* installments before it did, so, too, does the *X* series offer a challenge to skilled players, but, while they are difficult, they don't revel in causing psychological harm to the player (unlike the bastard games on pages 138, 139, and 146).

Since pen-and-paper games like *Dungeons and Dragons* require no technology to speak of, they could become as elaborate as desired, often utilizing fantasy settings to provide gamers with fantastic worlds to play around in. Hironobu Sakaguchi took inspiration from these tabletop activities to create what was to be his swan song, but instead became the biggest success of his career: *Final Fantasy*. The original *Final Fantasy* offered players a huge, dangerous, *exciting* world to explore. It also had some degree of character customization, which was pretty much unheard of at the time. *Final Fantasy* managed to not only reinvigorate Sakaguchi's career and love of making games, it helped propagate role-playing video games.

As with most successful properties, sequels and spin-offs soon began flying out of the original *Final Fantasy*. While many excellent titles bear the *FF* name, *Final Fantasy III* (or *Final Fantasy VI* in Japan) is often considered the best of the main series. It's so highly detailed, so painstakingly crafted, and so much fun that you could spend decades scouring it and never find every secret to be unlocked.

---

[91] Although *Mega Man 8* did have the bonus of having some incredibly cheesy anime cutscenes added in, with voice acting so bad it was a laugh riot. Dr. Light's performance is of particular note, with his VA often stumbling over his lines and mispronouncing names, like the dreaded "Doctah Wahwee."

While the story begins as a basic tale of scrappy rebels rising up against a tyrannical empire, it ends up becoming an epic tale of friendship, loneliness, and bravery. *Final Fantasy III*'s many characters are three-dimensional beings, a stark contrast to the cookie-cutter heroes of most early RPGs, each with their own hopes, fears, and story arcs to deal with, and more than a few special abilities for the less thematically minded players to enjoy.

FF III's primary antagonist, Kefka, provides a marvelous example on how to reverse an audience's expectations in order to tell a better story. He begins the game as a bit of a joke, serving the wizened Emperor Gestahl while garbed in a garishly bright (not to mention poofy) clown suit. But, like Vader before him, Kefka destroys his master. He then goes on to reveal the layers of dark depths to his personality; he may start the story as a walking punchline, but through his madness and his hate, he becomes a literal god for the player to defeat. *Final Fantasy III*'s narrative initially seems straightforward, but when Kefka takes hold of the narrative, things take a turn into crazy town and what was a typical RPG becomes an open-world apocalyptic fantasy.

Imagine if you had the chance to travel history. Would you use this power to check out eras that have long since passed or yet to have happened? Would you watch the Big Bang and hang out at the End of Time? Or would you pop back to last week to make sure your significant other doesn't hear you call their mom a bitch? If your name is Crono, you'll probably end up banding together with a bunch of multi-talented, multi-temporal friends and put a halt to that nasty end of the world thing.

Thirteen Video Game Bosses Who Laugh At Your Pitiful Attempts to Defeat Them[92]

Boss fights are a key element of nearly any game; they give the player a benchmark of accomplishment, as well as being a measure of their skill. While most of these battles are designed for players to emerge triumphant without too much stress, there are those few bosses designed to push players to their limits and suss out teh H@rdc0re from teh noobs. These bosses aren't just hard, they're downright evil.

 | CULEX

Game: *Super Mario RPG*

---

[92] Yes, I'm sure some of you guys are super-badasses, who took down every single one of these bosses your first try. Well, for the rest of us, they were all a real pain in the ass.

12 | TABUU

Game: *Super Smash Bros. Brawl*

11 | SEPHIROTH

Game: *Kingdom Hearts*

10 & **9** | THE EMERALD AND RUBY WEAPONS

Game: *Final Fantasy VII*

8 | C'THUN

Game: *World of Warcraft*

7 | PRETTY MUCH ANY FINAL BOSS FROM A KING OF FIGHTERS GAME[93]

Series: *King of Fighters*

6 | ALMA

Game: *Ninja Gaiden*

5 | WIEGRAF (RIOVANES CASTLE)

Game: *Final Fantasy Tactics*

4 | DEVIL EYE

Series: *Mega Man*

3 | RODIN

Game: *Bayonetta*

2 | THE FLAMELURKER

Game: *Demon's Souls*

1 | QUEEN LARSA

Game: *Mushihimesama Futari*

---

[93] Man, what is it with fighting games having such obnoxious final bosses? Seems like they're always cheaters, too. *King of the Fighters* is definitely the worst offender in this category, though, with bastards like Goenitz and his full-screen projectiles and non-stop assault of insanely damaging combos.

We gamers may like to argue about a lot of things—*Terrans are so OP! You guys better nerf Irelia! Get Tom Nook off my back about those damn payments!*—but *Chrono Trigger* is that effortlessly likable kid in school, the one virtually no one dislikes.[94] Its characters are a memorable bunch, the story engages players on an emotional level, the fast-paced gameplay never grows old, and the music! Yasunori Mitsuda gave us one of the strongest soundtracks you'll ever hear—every single flipping tune in *Chrono Trigger* is a fudging masterpiece. If you check out *Chrono Trigger* remixes online, you'll find that there are *hundreds* of them. When your source material is this creative, it helps beget creativity out of other people.

What began as an unusual alliance between Squaresoft and Nintendo ended up creating one of the greatest games in history— *Super Mario RPG*. Like *Chrono Trigger*, *Super Mario RPG* has an awesome score that sticks with you long after you've put the controller down. It's an active RPG for its day, too. You roam 3-D environments, and in combat you'll attack and defend against enemies through the use of precise button pressing. The days of hammering A to tell all of your characters to attack were a long-gone experience. *Mario RPG* holds up well today thanks to this focus on action and its frequent, but well-balanced, battles—you won't have to waste precious hours running around the same areas over and over to gain the power you need to progress.

---

[94] And those who do dislike it are wrong, as well as being poopy poopheads.

Though *Metroid*[95] and *Metroid II* were both great, *Super Metroid* firmly ensconced the franchise as one of gaming's most celebrated. *Super Metroid* stars bounty hunter Samus Aran as she traverses the depths of planet Zebes, and during your adventure you're free to explore wherever, whenever, with the only limit being your skills and abilities. *Super Metroid* defined the mood of the series by providing the player with a spooky, claustrophobic, and often lonely experience as they explore this alien world. Samus is by herself on Zebes, with only her wits and kick-ass power suit to guide her. *Super Metroid*'s gloomy aesthetic and haunting music bring to mind the *Alien* films, though the player can rest easy knowing that any Xenomorph foolish enough to burst forth to attack Samus will find that to be the *last* thing it ever does. Any hopeful game-makers should study every second of *Super Metroid*, as it uses subtle, in-game moments to letting the player educate his or herself rather than assault them with exposition and explanatory text boxes.

According to beat 'em ups, the '90s were a dangerous era, filled with gangs of thugs whose only purpose in life was to hassle the good citizens and vandalize anything they could get their hands on. Fortunately, there were always a couple of strong-willed and stronger-fisted folks like Axel and his buddies willing to take out these vagabonds. Like Wolverine, the *Streets of Rage* series is the best at what it does: let the player beat the crap out of some no-goodniks. *Streets of Rage 2* is widely considered the best in the *Rage* series, thanks to it offering players a wide variety of moves with which to pummel the bad guys, a lot of cool locations to administer said beatdowns, and a wide variety of baddies hungry for knuckle sandwiches. Yuzo Koshiro's score makes full use of the odd little sound chip in the Sega Genesis, creating music so blood-pumpingly catchy you'll often find yourself bobbing your head as you punch some faces.

In the '90s, every hero had a 'tude.[96] I'm talking attitude, yo, and nobody was more tude-acious than Sonic the Hedgehog. Fortunately, Sonic's games had a fun factor to match his swagger, with fast-paced plat-

---

[95] *Metroid* is one of the oldest games to have any kind of a twist ending to it. Once the player completed the game they were greeted with a congratulatory screen featuring *Metroid*'s hero, Samus, taking off his helmet to reveal—surprise! He is actually a she! Woooah. Talk about getting Shyamalan'd.

[96] Except for Mario. He's always been polite and cheerful, that little rapscallion.

forming action set in huge, secret-laden levels.

Each of the early *Sonic* titles introduced something new, such as Tails (who could be controlled by a second player), new items, new abilities, and Sonic's playable rival-turned-buddy, Knuckles. Many of the recent *Sonic* titles focus a little too much on mind-melting speed and Sonic's (sometimes) stupid menagerie of friends to remember to make the games, you know, *fun*. Sure, the original games don't lack in the speed department, but they also require some skilled navigation of their many lava reefs, mystic caves, and angel islands. And as with many of the other games in this book, the music in the original *Sonic* games is mighty fine. There's a reason Sonic was Sega's mascot, and Mario's only true rival, and it's because his games were unique and friggin' fun.

Millennial Masterpieces: Games that Rocked the Casbah During the Turn of the Millennium

While *Castlevania* was originally a platforming action/adventure game, *Castlevania: Symphony of the Night* transitioned the series into the "Metroidvania" format it's known for today. *Symphony of the Night* focuses on letting the player explore and revel in watching his or her powers grow over the course of the game. Though you're initially poorly armed and relatively powerless, once you're nearing the end of the game you'll be a super-jumping, spell-casting, shapeshifting menace to the forces of evil.

Symphony of the Night has a twist to it that audiences (at the time) never saw coming. When most players close in on having "100% completion" according to the in-game menu, what they don't know is that they're not almost finished ... *they're less than halfway through the game*. Suddenly they'll find that the map they'd thought they'd explored, and the world they've come to know, was only *half* of what's really out there. There are so many tucked away little alcoves and hidden bits of treasure and magic to be found that people are *still* finding new secrets even today.

Reboot. As I mentioned in the movies chapter, it's a dirty word in the geek world. Often reboots are mishandled cash grabs trying to make a quick buck based on the loyalty of an established fanbase, handled by folks who don't understand what it was that made the original franchise so great.[97] Sometimes, though, we geeks get lucky. Sometimes a reboot gets handled by a team of people who just *understands* it, and we end up getting something that keeps the spirit of the original, while adding some great new ideas to the

---

[97] We're looking at you, *DmC* and *Metroid: Other M*.

mix. *Metroid Prime* is one such title. The gaming world scoffed at the thought of the beloved 2D franchise suddenly shifting to the third dimension, but when *Prime* landed on Gamecubes around the globe, the scoffing ceased. Here we had the same kind of lonesome, extraterrestrial adventures we'd had before, but transformed into something new for modern fans to enjoy.

Video games are often about empowerment; for some reason, players enjoy the feeling of being an awesome badass. The *Devil May Cry* series took this idea and ran with it. On the surface, it's a 3D action game with an emphasis on swordplay and gothic horror. But if you dig deeper, you'll find that the *Devil May Cry* titles are really about having fun and showing off. Protagonist Dante doesn't just fight demons, he fights them with *style,* and enjoys every minute of it.

GEEK
Spotlight

Lucca Ashtear

*"Machines aren't capable of evil. **Humans** make them that way."*

It's a good thing *Chrono Trigger*'s Crono ended up being pals with a genius engineer, seeing as how he ends up sucked into a time vortex and all ... of course, neither of them would have been sucked into that time vortex in the first place if it wasn't for her, so I guess it all evens out. Still, that minor snafu aside, Lucca's a heck of a gal. She's one of history's greatest geniuses, able to explain the physics behind time travel, manufacture handy-dandy combat gadgets, and get an advanced robot working despite the fact that he's from thousands of years in the future. She's no dry bookworm, however. Lucca's a gabber, always ready with a light-hearted joke, which is probably why her best friend is a mute, red-headed swordsman.

Stuntman/voice actor Reuben Langdon is predominantly associated with the role of Dante, having provided the motion capture for him in several games and voicing him in several titles, and he portrays such gleeful swagger in the demon hunter that it's damn near impossible for any gamer not to have fun.

Massively Multiplayer Online Gaming: Discovering a You That's Digital, but with a 500 DPS Flaming Longsword

While most video games are a two-way conversation between gamers and the content creators, online games are huge, multi-headed hydras of communication between gamers, the creators, and *other* gamers. As with real human interactions, adding this extra human element to gaming can make it occasionally frustrating, often fun, and always different.

There are many, *many* MMOs out there (which we'll discuss later), but the common element to all of them is how much effort they put into creating a cohesive, *living* world for the player to have adventures in. There's a limited lifespan to most games—you start them, you finish them, and the game's over. Maybe there'll be some competitive multiplayer to keep your interest for a while, or maybe there'll be some downloadable content down the line to give you a little more bang for your buck, but eventually things wind down and come to an end. With MMOs, however, the adventure doesn't end until the game's creators decide to pull the plug. To put things in perspective, *Ultima Online* and *Everquest* are two of the first expansive MMOs out there, and they're still going strong fifteen years later.

Like any piece of art, a perfectly crafted video game becomes something more than its components—it can be an uplifting, emotional[98] experience. A well-crafted MMO provides a new type of home for its players. Ask anyone who's been playing *World of Warcraft* since the old days and they'll probably tell you that some of the best buds they've ever had were online. Someone who is shy in the real world can be as brave as they want to be online because it's a *safe* environment. Likewise, many who suffer physical handicaps enjoy playing MMOs because they're a way to interact with others without having their handicap come into play.[99]

---

[98] And I don't mean emotional as in it makes you cry like the women on *Maury* who discover that the twentieth guy they brought on the show isn't their baby's daddy. I mean emotional as in it makes you feel those wonderful feels, bro, whether they're sad, happy, amazed, or nostalgic.

[99] Penny Arcade's *Extra Credits* series stated the wonderful inclusiveness offered in games in the episode "Toxicity," stating that: "Games are a place where all of society's standards fall away, where we agree on a shared reality that we craft to be better than this one, where everyone can be seen for their strengths and not their weaknesses. It's a place where a child in a wheelchair can run, where the awkward or shy can communicate, where the frightened can be brave. It's a place where we can be colorblind, free from assumptions and deaf to our differences."

Twelve Lies Video Games Taught Me

12 | Driving over arrows will make your car go faster.

11 | Broken objects and dead/unconscious people flash a few times and disappear.

10 | You'll be healed by eating ham or turkeys you discover on the ground, in trash cans, or inside brick walls.

9 | Merely *touching* a medical kit is enough to recover you from even the most dire of wounds.

8 | Anything red explodes when shot. Red barrels? Pow! Red crates? Bang! That cow you painted red? Moo-BOOM!

7 | Never discard anything you pick up—it could come in handy later.

6 | You can smash blocks by jumping head first into them.

5 | It's perfectly acceptable to go inside someone's house, rummage through their stuff, smash their pots, and then maybe talk to them if you feel like it.

4 | You can get away with any amount of crime so long as you repaint your car.

3 | Handguns may need to be reloaded occasionally, but they'll never run out of ammo.

2 | A cardboard box is all you need to hide from bad guys.

1 | No matter how open things seem, if you walk far enough, you'll run into an invisible wall.

Five Old-School Video Game Levels
So Hard You Might Choke Somebody

5 | *Mike Tyson's Punch-Out* (NES) – The Battle Against Mike Tyson

4 | *Teenage Mutant Ninja Turtles* (NES) – That damn Dam Level

3 | *The Lion King* (SNES) – The Ostrich Level

2 | *Little Nemo: The Dream Master* (NES) – House of Toys

1 | *Battletoads* (NES) – The Hoverbike Tunnel

MMOs can also be strange little microcosms that reflect the real world, with all its quirks, oddness, and awfulness.

Quirky, Odd, and Somewhat Awful MMOments

THE ASSASSINATION OF LORD BRITISH BY THE COWARD RAINZ
Game: *Ultima Online*

Ultima Online subscribes to a typical fantasy monarchy, and at the head of that monarchy sits Lord British, the invulnerable in-game avatar of *Ultima* creator Richard Garriott. While it's true that no weapon forged could harm the king, this was an early PC game, and with it came clunky implementation of in-game features—the king's invulnerability had to be manually activated every time Garriott logged in. After the game's servers crashed, Garriott forgot to re-invulnablize Lord British, and a player named Rainz seized this opportunity and slayed the previously unslayable king, firing gossip shockwaves across the internet and securing his place in history as a legendary griefer.[100]

THE PANDEMIC PLAGUE OF AZEROTH
Game: *World of Warcraft*

MMOs receive constant updates and expansions to help keep their playerbases happy, and one of *World of Warcraft*'s updates introduced a boss Troll with a plague attack which not only

---

[100] Griefer: a player who isn't playing the same game you are, they're playing a meta-game wherein the goal is to piss you and everyone else off as much as possible.

infected its target, but the players around him/her. Soon wily players figured out how to bring this plague with them out of the boss's dungeon and into the rest of the world, and a pandemic swept across Azeroth. Low-level players died in droves to this damaging plague, and friendly NPCs, while invulnerable to the damaging effects, could still carry the disease, which meant that they each acted as a virtual Typhoid Mary to anyone who had the misfortune of going near them. The once highly populated capital cities were the first to go, eventually becoming sickness-riddled wastelands that few were brave enough to traverse. Eventually Blizzard, the makers of *World of Warcraft*, had to step in and repeatedly update/patch/restart their game servers until the final traces of the plague had been eliminated. Oddly enough, this virtual plague spread similarly to the way real disease spreads—Doctors and bioterrorism specialists have examined this incident as a means of better understanding real-world viral outbreaks.

EVE ONLINE'S PONZI SCHEME

Game: *EVE Online*

For the uninitiated, a Ponzi scheme[101] is a scam wherein investors get roped in, falsely promised big profits, and are instead paid with their own investment capital or the investment capital of subsequent investors. At the top lies the scammer, who eventually takes off with a boatload of money after the investments have hit critical mass.

EVE Online offers sci-fi MMO gaming with a twist: players can invest and make real money from it. While pulling off a real-life Ponzi scheme will get your butt thrown in jail, the perpetrators of *EVE Online*'s massive scam got no such reprimand because they'd scammed people within a virtual environment. Their premise was simple: give them your money, and in a single week you'd get your money back, with an additional five percent interest. It's a classic con built around that classic con premise—make the mark think he's the one ripping *you* off by offering him something too good to be true. Well, it *was* too good to be true, and once their wealth hit a critical mass, they struck like money-grubbing lightning and made off with virtual assets worth fifty *thousand* dollars of real money. You heard me. Fifty K. 50,000 smackers. That'll buy you a lotta chimichangas. They got away with it, too, despite those meddling kids,[102] and used their ill-gotten gains to do God-knows what. If they're smart, they retired on some virtual beach somewhere, clinking virtual margaritas together while their virtual butlers bring their virtual yacht around.

Quick Hits

There are a lot of great games out there perfect for any geeks hungry to grab a controller and start playing. While I can't possibly hope to list all of them, here are some

---

[101] Named after Charles Ponzi, who didn't invent the scam, but he made it famous by making a ton of money doing it and then getting caught.
[102] And their dog, too!

quickies I've yet to mention, all arranged by category, with little tidbits as to why you might want to play them if you've never had the pleasure. Also, know that I'm going to frequently be referring to video game *series* here, rather than individual titles, so when I say you should play *Diablo, Fallout, or Xtreme Chiropractor Quest: The Journey to Subluxation Mountain,*[103] I'm not only talking about the first ones.

Role-Playing Games of the Wild Wild West...ern Part of the Hemisphere

- *Fallout.* Open-ended post-apocalyptic fun with a frequently off-beat sense of humor.
- *Diablo.* The archetypal dungeon crawler. You pick a character, fight monsters, grab loot, and try to survive as you go deeper and deeper into the dark, dank depths.
- *Torchlight. Diablo's* friendly first cousin, now with puppies and kitties!
- *Star Wars: Knights of the Old Republic.* Third edition Dungeons and Dragons rules and freedom combined with a smart story, interesting characters, and a *Star Wars* setting.
- *Mass Effect.* An original sci-fi universe with great characters, pleasing combat, and a third entry which left much of the fanbase friggin' furious.
- *X-Com: Enemy Unknown.* Tough-as-nails turn-based tactical game where you'll have to diligently allocate resources and command your troops in battle or the aliens will crush you between their spindly gray fingers.
- *Baldur's Gate 2: Shadows of Amn.* Sharply written and almost endless adventures await in this 2nd edition Dungeons and Dragons-based game.
- *Arcanum: Of Steamworks & Magick Obscura.* Similar to *Baldur's Gate* and the first two *Fallouts,* only with a steampunk edge.
- *Dungeon Siege I* and *II.* Dungeon crawling fun with parties of up to eight characters such as fighters, mages, and donkeys.

Role-Playing Games from the Far, Far East

- *Pokémon.* Collect monsters, train them, and duke it out to prove that you're the very best, like no one ever was.

---

[103] Although you can skip *Xtreme Chiropractor Quest IV: The Return of Dark Lord D.D. Palmer.* It's just not up to snuff when compared to the rest of the *Xtreme Chiropractor Quest* series.

- *Etrian Odyssey.* Rich rewards await gamers brave enough to confront this often-unforgiving RPG.
- *Dragon Quest/Warrior.* Old-school fun with little to no new-school trappings bogging it down (or making your life any easier).
- *Final Fantasy,* especially *Final Fantasy VI, VII, IX, XII,* and *Final Fantasy Tactics.*
- *Robotrek.* Build robots and beat up other robots. 'Nuff said.
- *Earthbound.* Many try, but few games succeed in being so quirky, funny, and full of character as this classic SNES RPG.

Free Time is for Wimps: Massively Multiplayer Online Games

- *World of Warcraft. WoW* is one of the biggest MMOs in the world, and it's because it offers constant updates, tons of activities for players to do, and panda people.
- *Everquest, Ultima Online, Dark Age of Camelot.* Three fantasy MMOs that helped crack open the flood gates for all MMOs to follow.
- *Star Wars: The Old Republic.* It's similar to *Knights of the Old Republic,* only you play it online with a billion other Jedi and Boba Fett wannabes.
- *DC Universe Online.* One of the few superhero MMOs remaining, and it has the benefit of having the entire DC universe to play around in to boot.
- *Marvel Heroes.* This free-to-play title offers gameplay like *Diablo,* but updates like an MMO, and has in-game items and characters priced like they're made of ever-lovin' platinum.
- *EVE Online.* Intricate sci-fi MMO about spaceships and corporate extortion.
- *Rift.* Borrows heavily from the advancements of *World of Warcraft,* but leans toward letting players customize their characters and pore over minute bonuses to figure out which provides the .3% advantage over the others.
- *Guild Wars.* Unlike most MMOs, these fast-paced RPGs ask no subscription fee, only that you buy the base copy of the game and send them some sweet honey kisses to show your appreciation.

Kick, Punch, It's All in the Mind: Fighting Games

- *Super Smash Bros.* Up to four can play as Nintendo's greatest characters and beat the crap out of each other. It don't get much better than this, people.
- *Street Fighter Alpha 3.* Large cast, flexible fighting system that can be customized to fit your style of play, and more game modes than you can shake R. Mika's ponytails at.
- *Street Fighter III: Third Strike.* A precise, yet colorful and accessible, fighting game often considered one of, if not *the,* best of its genre.
- *Super Street Fighter IV Arcade Edition.* A slower, more thoughtful fighter for those who aren't as inclined toward frantic button presses.
- *Ultimate Mortal Kombat 3 & Mortal Kombat 9.* These two are often considered the best in this bloody, fatality-filled franchise.
- *Marvel Vs. Capcom.* A huge cast of characters spanning both companies' impressive history, and gameplay so fast and flashy you might have a seizure.
- *Skullgirls.* Impressively animated, hand-drawn 2D fighter with a tightly balanced cast of scantily clad characters who play hopscotch with the line between being cloyingly cheesecake and outright misogynistic.
- *Tekken.* 3D combat with a wide cast of crazy combatants such as robots, pandas, and dudes made of wood.
- *Soul Calibur.* Sort of like *Tekken,* but with heavily armed medieval warriors, and Darth Vader.
- *Darkstalkers.* Sort of like if *Street Fighter* had kids with a bunch of B-movie monsters.

Ten Games So Bad They Might Kill You

As with anything geeky, video games come in both amazing and awful packages. I've spent a while extolling the values of most of the greatest games the medium has to offer, but I'd be remiss if I didn't also mention some of the stinkers, so that you, gentle gamer, know which ones to avoid.

10 | *E.T.: The Extra Terrestrial* (Atari)

9 | *Shaq-Fu* (Sega Genesis)

8 | *Bubsy 3D* (Playstation)

7 | Any of those god-awful *Link* CD-i games

6 | *Big Rigs: Over the Road Racing* (PC)

5 | *Aquaman* (Gamecube/Xbox)

4 | *Final Fantasy: All the Bravest* (iOS)

3 | *The War Z* (PC)

2 | *Custer's Revenge* (Atari)

1 | *Superman 64* (Nintendo 64)

 Platonic Platformers

- *DuckTales.* Help Scrooge McDuck explore the world and make sure his money stays where it belongs—with him!
- *Rocket Knight Adventures.* A possum with a laser blade and a jetpack fights armies of evil pigs. If you need something more to sell you on this game, I don't know what to tell you.
- *Kirby Super Star.* One tough cream puff goes around clobbering bad guys in a variety of gameplay modes, fighting bosses and copying enemy powers, all while looking super adorable.

- *Ristar.* Great animation, fantastic music, fun locales, and even funner-er aliens to bop.
- *Psychonauts.* Great writing and cool psychokinetic powers keep this 3D platformer feeling fresh, even though it's set in a summer camp full of (presumably) stinky kids.
- *Banjo Kazooie.* Glorious 3D platforming action from the Nintendo 64 era, so it's got about 4 frames per second and the textures all look like mud, but by *Odin's beard* is it good.
- *Super Meat Boy.* Blisteringly fast, *incredibly* difficult gameplay that will rip out your duodenum and slap you in the face with it if you're not ready.

It's a Whole Open World (Don't Dare Close Your Eyes)

- *Grand Theft Auto* (anything from *GTA 3* onward is solid). Essentially created the open-world genre, allowing players to run around and do *whatever.* Run over hookers, shoot cops, go bowling, be a firefighter, go to the gym—you can do it all!
- *Red Dead Redemption.* Sort of like *Grand Theft Auto*, but in cowboy times, and you're more of a good guy.[104]
- *Saint's Row.* Sort of like *Grand Theft Auto*, but jacked up on a combination of crystal meth, Red Bull, and your cousin Stevie's ADD medication.
- *Batman: Arkham City, Spider-Man 2*, and *The Incredible Hulk: Ultimate Destruction.* Each game captures the essence of what would be fun about being Batman, The Incredible Hulk, and Spider-Man, respectively. For Batman, it's skulking around intimidating bad guys and beating the crap out of them. For Spidey, it's webslinging around New York. For Hulk, it's smashing stuff.

---

[104] In the cutscenes, at least. Outside of the cutscenes, you can hogtie a woman and leave her in front of an oncoming train if you want. You even get an achievement for it called "Dastardly."

- *Prototype.* Contains much of the same soaring, smashing fun of *Hulk: Ultimate Destruction*, but in a gorier, sci-fi/horror package.
- *State of Decay.* Live through the zombie apocalypse by banding together with other survivors, fighting for supplies, establishing/upgrading a home base, and generally being a badass zombie slayer.
- *Crackdown.* Play as a supercop and leap around the city punching bad dudes in their bad faces.
- *The Elder Scrolls V: Skyrim.* Huge, Norse-inspired world to explore, filled with magic, dragons, and danger. Also, as I mentioned before, you can *shout a bear off of a friggin' mountain.*
- *Far Cry 3: Blood Dragon.* Free-roaming fun in an insane future world that resembles what people in the '80s thought the future would be, which is to say that it's filled with laser lights, cyborgs, and VHSes.

Shoot-Em-Up/Run-And-Gun

- *Gunstar Heroes.* Mix and match power-ups with a buddy while you shoot down countless bad guys.
- *Contra.* It's tough to make it through this old-school shooter, but it'll make a hero out of you, and it's one of the few games where it's recommended that you cheat.
- *Gradius III.* Fly a spaceship, snag powerups, and shoot Easter Island heads.
- *Ikaruga.* Fly a spaceship, switch between black and white polarities depending on what color enemies you're facing, ponder whether the game has racist undertones.

Really Timely and Strategic: Real-Time Strategy

- *Age of Empires.* Manage medieval villages and conquer other empires made up of people who look similar to you, but speak a slightly different language.
- *Age of Mythology.* Sort of like *Age of Empires*, but if you could also create mythological monsters like Anubites, scorpion men, and laser bears.
- *Empire Earth.* Sort of like *Age of Empires*, but if you could begin the

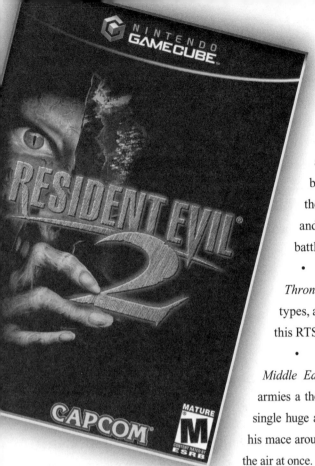

game as cavemen and end it in a futuristic city armed with mechs and nanomachines.

• *Starcraft: Brood War* and *Starcraft II*. These tightly balanced sci-fi strategy title pits the grotesque Zerg, proud Protoss, and Terrans (a.k.a. humans) in a battle for supremacy.

• *Warcraft III: The Frozen Throne*. Four races, countless game types, and an incredible map editor give this RTS almost endless possibilities.

• *Lord of the Rings: The Battle for Middle Earth II*. Massive battles between armies a thousand men strong, or between a single huge army and friggin' Sauron waving his mace around and knocking twenty dudes in the air at once.

The Horror, The Horror: Horror Games

- *Alone in the Dark*. This progenitor of the survival horror genre may be low on graphical power, but it's high on atmosphere and spookiness.
- *Resident Evil* (Especially *2, 3,* and *4*). Zombies, mutants, and a bleached-blonde dude with sunglasses all try to make chum out of you and your chums.
- *Silent Hill 1, 2,* and *3*. It's like Hell, but only if Hell was a small Midwest town filled with disturbing, psychologically inspired horrors.
- *Slender*. Collect eight pages to unlock the secret of Slenderman, the modern boogeyman with a nice suit and a penchant for child-stealing.

- *Amnesia: Dark Descent.* Face Lovecraftian horrors while grappling with the fact that you can't fight back, and that you were going to go to bed two hours ago, but lost track of time.

You Shouldn't Have Done That: Creepy Video Game Urban Legends

Interestingly enough, horror games aren't the only source of video game horror. Urban legends have long been a staple of American culture, ever since the first mischievous uncle told his impressionable nieces and nephews about the couple who were attacked by a hook-handed man.[105] Since video games are both a solitary experience when played, and a social experience when discussed with others, that makes them perfect fodder for some video game-related urban legends.[106]

Urban Legend: Pokémon Black
Source Game: *Pokémon*, first-generation
After finding this ebony cartridge at a flea market, the player found that it seemed to be "haunted" by a ghost pokémon that followed him around and couldn't be removed. The spectral cohort also granted him the ability to unwittingly *kill* other pokémon trainers and their pokémon. After beating the game, he was confronted by the memories of all the beings he'd slain, and his ghostly companion turned on him, forcing him to fight it. He couldn't hurt the ghost, or escape. Eventually it defeats him and the screen goes black, then erases its save data.

Urban Legend: You Shouldn't Have Done That ... (Ben Drowned)
Source Game: *The Legend of Zelda: Majora's Mask*
The player receives a mysterious, mislabeled copy of *The Legend of Zelda: Majora's Mask*, as per usual, and the game is terrifying and messed up, repeatedly taunting him with a creepy Link statue and the message, "You shouldn't have done that ..." As he continues to play, he keeps dying no matter what he does, and finds that the in-game characters and world seem stricken with some supernatural malaise. What sets this tale apart is that, not only did the player write a string of forum posts detailing his experience, he uploaded several *videos* of him "playing" the haunted game, all of which are still available online.

---

[105] The only things we know about the original hook hand is that he loved his mother very dearly, was a member of army, and would often howl, "I'M A MONSTEEEER!"

[106] Most of these are commonly known as "creepypasta" on the internet, due to the fact that they're often creepy stories that readers can cut and past. And that, whenever you read one, you'll always end up eating a bowl of pasta afterwards.

Urban Legend: Sonic.exe

Source Game: *Sonic the Hedgehog*

The story goes that the player received a copy of *Sonic the Hedgehog* in the mail, sent to him by his friend, Kyle, along with a stern warning to destroy the disc (which makes you wonder why Kyle went to the trouble of *mailing* it instead of destroying it himself.) Regardless, in this ghastly version of *Sonic the Hedgehog*, the player was forced to play as either Tails, Knuckles, or Dr. Robotnik while being chased down by an evil version of Sonic. He can't escape, and whenever he loses, the character becomes unplayable. Once he ran out of lives, the screen went berserk and filled with a giant, hyper-realistic picture of this devilfied Sonic and the message, "I AM GOD."

Urban Legend: Herobrine

Source Game: *Minecraft*

A *Minecraft* player creates a single-player world in which to build things and go on adventures, but notices a player-esque being barely at the edge of his vision. Thinking it a glitch, he continues playing, and as does, he notices things that shouldn't be there—tunnels carved out of mountains, harvested plants, oddly stacked formations of earth and rock. He tries to check the *Minecraft* forums about this mysterious character, but no-one has heard anything ... but he does receive a private message from one forum-goer, named Herobrine, with the message, STOP. As he investigates deeper, he finds out that *Minecraft*'s creator, Notch, had a brother who played the game quite a bit. But he died a few months ago.
And his username was Herobrine.[107]

Urban Legend: Killswitch[108]

Source Game: *Killswitch*

This Russian puzzle game took place in a factory filled with demons, and was unsolvable due to both its mind-bending riddles and the fact that it would uninstall itself to screw with the player's head.

Urban Legend: MARIO

Source Game: *Super Mario World*

In this tale, the player downloads a mysterious, oddly labeled hack of *Super Mario World*, one that paints Mario as the antagonist, and is filled with the tortured scrawls of seemingly murdered souls.

---

[107] And he's RIGHT BEHIND YOU!

[108] Not to be confused with *Kill.Switch*, which is a very real video game by Namco.

Urban Legend: Polybius

Source Game: *Polybius*

In the 1980s, this intense, Tempest-esque arcade game would infect the minds of any who played it, leading to insomnia, nightmares, amnesia, and suicidal tendencies. Allegedly, there were men in black who collected "data" from the machines, though no one knows why.

Ten Video Game Urban Legends That, While Not Creepy, Still Plagued the Heck Outta Gamers[109]

10 | Bringing Aeris back to life. - *Final Fantasy VII*

9 | Finding Bigfoot. - *Grand Theft Auto: San Andreas*

8 | Playing as Luigi (L is real 2401). - *Super Mario 64*

7 | Obtaining the Triforce. - *The Legend of Zelda: Ocarina of Time*

6 | Obtaining Mew. - *Pokémon Red/Blue*

5 | Fighting Sheng Long. - *Street Fighter II*

4 | Fighting/unlocking/seeing/having brunch with Ermac. - *Mortal Kombat*

3 | Unlocking Sonic and Tails. - *Super Smash Bros. Melee*

2 | The secret cow level. - *Diablo*[110]

1 | The face on the moon/secret door outline. - *Final Fantasy II (IV)*

---

[109] I'm not going to list the various methods by which people claimed to be able to complete these urban legends because 1. They're all wrong. 2. There were dozens of methods per legend. 3. They all amounted to the same basic formula: waste a ton of time doing something that's a huge pain in the ass.

[110] Oddly enough, several of these urban legends were so prolific that the games' developers threw in references to them in sequels, such as Ermac becoming a playable character in later *Mortal Kombat* titles, or *Diablo II*'s secret level filled with demonic cows. And yes, that's a real level, not just some goofy thing I threw in for laughs.

Miscellaneous Greatness

Here are a few games that don't really fit in any of the previously mentioned categories but are still worthwhile entries into any gamer's library, whether you're the most hardcore of gaming gods or nubile of nascent noobs.

Shadow of the Colossus (action/adventure), *Plants vs. Zombies* (tower defense), *Fez* (mind-bending platformer), *Maniac Mansion* and its followup, *Maniac Mansion: Day of the Tentacle, Sam and Max Hit the Road* (point and click), *Burnout 3: Takedown* (racing/crashing) *Metal Gear Solid* (tactical espionage action), *Pac-Man, Pac-Man: Championship Edition DX, Galaga, Tetris,* (score-based games) *Critter Crunch* (puzzle/score-based game), *Goldeneye 007,*[111] *Doom, Quake, Gears of War, Halo,* (first/third-person shooters).

Twenty Five Phrases Only Gamer Geeks Will Fully Appreciate

25 | The cake is a lie. – *Portal*

24 | Winners don't use drugs. – *Pretty much every arcade game in the '90s*

23 | Do a barrel roll! – *Starfox 64*

22 | Welcome to die! – *X-Men: The Arcade Game*

21 | Hey! Listen! – *The Legend of Zelda: Ocarina of Time*

20 | LEEEEROY JENKINS! – *World of Warcraft*

19 | You spoony bard! – *Final Fantasy II (IV)*

---

[111] Which is often colloquially referred to as *Goldeneye 64*.

18 | Get over here! – *Mortal Kombat*

17 | Go home and be a family man. – *Street Fighter II*

16 | Falcon ... PAWNCH! – *Super Smash Bros.*

15 | Waluigi time! – *Mario Kart: Double Dash*

14 | You're Winner. – *Big Rigs: Over the Road Racing*

13 | My life for Aiur. – *Starcraft*

12 | I'm Commander Shepard and this is my favorite store on the Citadel. – *Mass Effect 2*

11 | Objection! – *Phoenix Wright: Ace Attorney*

10 | You were almost a Jill sandwich! – *Resident Evil*

9 | Call me a treasure hunter or I'll rip your lungs out! – *Final Fantasy III (VI)*

8 | Wise fwom youw gwave! – *Altered Beast*

7 | "Marry" me with my money. – *Sunset Riders*

6 | Heaven or Hell? LET'S ROCK! – *Guilty Gear*

5 | Ahh, fresh meat. – *Diablo*

4 | I'm selling these fine leather jackets. – *Monkey Island*

3 | Spy sappin' mah sentry! – *Team Fortress 2*

2 | Snake? SNAKE? SNAAAAAKE! – *Metal Gear Solid*

1 | Say, "Fuzzy pickles!" – *Earthbound*

Ten Video Game Characters with Character

As I've mentioned before, most video games aren't exactly known for their writing, or for their engaging characters—too often our heroes get relegated to being mute player avatars. Sometimes, however, game creators will put in some extra oomph when creating their characters, and we'll get heroes who are as much a joy to watch as they are to play as.

⑩ | NATHAN DRAKE

Series: *Uncharted*

Voice Actor: Nolan North

Occupation: Treasure hunter

Choice quote: "Great, power's out, and a girl's trapped. I swear to God, if there's a zombie around the next corner..."

⑨ | DANTE

Series: *Devil May Cry*

Voice Actor: Reuben Langdon

Occupation: Demon hunter

Choice quote: "This party's getting *crazy!*"

⑧ | SOLID SNAKE

Series: *Metal Gear Solid*

Voice Actor: David Hayter

Occupation: Spy

Choice quote: "Metal Gear?"

⑦ | ELES CHERE

Title: *Final Fantasy III (VI)*

Occupation: General

Choice quote: "I'm a general, not some opera floozy!"

6 | ANDREW RYAN

Title: *Bioshock*

Voice Actor: Armin Shimmerman

Occupation: Industrialist

Choice quote: "I am Andrew Ryan, and I'm here to ask you a question: is a man not entitled to the sweat of his brow? 'No!' says the man in Washington, 'It belongs to the poor.' 'No!' says the man in the Vatican, 'It belongs to God.' 'No!' says the man in Moscow, 'It belongs to everyone.' I rejected those answers; instead, I chose something different. I chose the impossible. I chose... *Rapture*, a city where the artist would not fear the censor, where the scientist would not be bound by petty morality, where the great would not be constrained by the small! And with the sweat of your brow, Rapture can become your city as well."

5 | BAYONETTA

Series: *Bayonetta*

Voice Actor: Helena Taylor

Occupation: Witch/detective

Choice quote: "I'm sorry, I forgot to mention one of the reasons I hunt your kind: you're much too ugly not to be taken out of your misery."

4 | ALYX VANCE

Series: *Half-life*

Voice Actor: Merle Dandridge

Occupation: Hacker

Choice quote: "Gordon, you know what'd be cool? Actually, I can't think of anything cooler than what just happened. Think it's dead? Maybe you should whack it with the crowbar just in case."

3 | ELIZABETH

Title: *Bioshock Infinite*

Voice Actor: Courtnee Draper

Occupation: Student

Choice quote: "Paris? Come on, let's go! Let's go right now!"

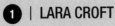 2 | CLOUD STRIFE

Series: *Final Fantasy*

Voice Actor: Steve Burton

Occupation: Ex-SOLDIER (Yes, it's all capitalized like that. In *Final Fantasy VII*, SOLDIERs are different from soldiers.)

Choice quote: "All right, everyone, let's mosey."

1 | LARA CROFT

Series: *Tomb Raider*

Voice Actor: Jonell Elliot, Shelly Blond, Judith Gibbons, Keely Hawes, and Camilla Luddington

Choice quote: "A famous explorer once said, that the extraordinary is in what we do, not who we are. I'd finally set out to make my mark, to find adventure. But instead adventure found me. In our darkest moments, when life flashes before us, we find something. Something that keeps us going. Something that pushes us. When all seemed lost, I found a truth. And I knew what I must become."

Some games that are terrible at least have the decency to wear their awfulness on their sleeves, like the games listed on page 151. Some games, however, seemed like they should be good—maybe they had big budgets, or great developers behind them, or were sequels to strong, established properties, but something about them just ain't right, which is why they left a trail of frustrated gamers in their wake.

Video Games So Disappointing People Almost Friggin' Rioted[112]

Metroid: Other M, DMC: Devil May Cry, Knights of the Old Republic II: The Sith Lords, Too Human, Aliens: Colonial Marines, SimCity (2013), *Fable 2* or *Fable 3*

---

[112] Note that I'm not necessarily saying that these games are all bad, they're just disappointing compared to the awesomeness we were expecting. Except for *DmC* and *Metroid: Other M*— those two games can burn in hell.

(depending on who you ask), *Teenage Mutant Ninja Turtles: Re-Shelled, Tony Hawk: Ride, Sonic the Hedgehog 4, Final Fantasy XIV, Resident Evil: Operation Raccoon City, Dragon Age II,* and *Ghostbusters: The Video Game.*

Honorary mention: The last ten minutes of *Mass Effect 3,* and *Diablo III's* unstable launch experience thanks to it only being playable if the player is connected to the internet.

Chapter 5

The Internet:

Why Sleep When You Could Be Watching People Blend iPhones?

S moke signals, carrier pigeons, and telephones—all steaming piles of crap compared to the informational power of the internet. Never before in human history has so much information been available to so many; anything you could ever want to learn is a mere keystroke away. So, naturally, most people spend their time on the 'net self-aggrandizing, acting like jerks to each other, or checking out pictures of cats doing silly things.

This goofy wad of weirdness we call the Web has changed the world and human interaction as we know it, altering the way we date, the way we acquire goods, and the way we brag about our most minute accomplishments. But I won't get too far into any of that. What I will get into, however, is how the net has provided unprecedented opportunities for creative types to do what they love. Thirty years ago, if you wanted to make a short film and have someone actually see it, you'd have to jump through a nearly infinite pile of flaming hoops to do so. Today, if you want someone to see your short film, all you have to do is go out and shoot the sucker and then post it online. *If you film it, they will come.*

Similarly, if you were interested in writing/drawing comics, you'd have to fight your way into a small, selective industry. But things have *changed.* Nowadays you can't throw a lemming without hitting a webcomic, and that's because the biggest measure of your success isn't who you know, it's how hard you're willing to work.

The Early Internet: The Dark Days of Message Boards and Dial-Up

The '90s internet was like a secret club located in a dark, dank alley. You might not find where you want to go, at first, but after putting in some time and learning whose hands to shake and which doors to take, you'd get where you needed to be. But, since the net was so lightly populated, you couldn't afford to be choosey about what sort of individuals you socialized with. Sometimes, this pushed folks together who might not have otherwise been friends. Sometimes it meant that you'd have to suffer through the incessant ramblings of some weirdo who was obsessed with Disney's *The Mighty Ducks.*[113]

It was a dark, strange era, to be sure, when the internet was first gaining popularity. In some ways it resembled the internet of today, but in a much more raw form. There wasn't Facebook or Twitter, but there were message boards devoted to your favorite topics. There wasn't Youtube, but that didn't stop the propagation of viral videos; I speak of the archaic proto-memes which surfaced in this ancient time, an era before Rage Comics and Advice Animals. Things such as *Star Wars Kid*, a video of a bespectacled teenager swinging a staff around as if to emulate a Jedi knight, and the *G.I. Joe Public Service Announcement Parodies*—comedic edits of the subtly strange public service announcements found at the end of each

---

[113] Not the movies, the cartoon series. I knew that guy, and, no matter what anyone was talking about, he'd always find a way to bring it back to the *Mighty* friggin' *Ducks*. Plans for the weekend? *Mighty Ducks*. What'd you have for breakfast? *Mighty Ducks*. How about all that apartheid? *Mighty Ducks*.

Five Quotes Only Internet Aficionados Will Fully Appreciate

5 | "All your base are belong to us." - The Sega Mega Drive game *Zero Wing*

4 | "Hey, kid. I'm a computer." - *GI Joe Parody Public Service Announcements*

3 | "Badgers, badgers, badgers, badgers, badgers, badgers, badgers, badgers, badgers, *badgers, badgers, badgers, mushroom MUSHROOM!*" - *Badger Badger Badger*

2 | "Hokay, so here's the Earth. 'Damn, that is a sweet Earth,' you might say." - *The End of the World*

1 | "The system is down." - *Strongbad*

episode of GI Joe—and lastly: the *Power Five,* ghastly images used to disgust the unwitting for the *schadenfreude* of their friends. If you know not who the Power Five are, do not search for them, or be prepared to bleach your eyes from your sockets. Members of the power five include Goatse, Tubgirl, and Lemon Party.[114]

Modern Internet: Expressing Yourself

Once download/upload speeds started to improve, we began to see more and more people taking to the web as a means of expression. Modern creative types take for granted their unprecedented ability to gain popularity as a content creator, and their ability to profit through sheer force-of-will. Before the internet, any aspiring film-makers, artists, or writers had to work their butts off and face rejection on a daily basis, all in the hopes that they'd be noticed by someone with some clout and money. Thanks to services like Youtube, the social networks, and Deviant Art, we creatives can find the audience hungry for our content.

Don't get me wrong; starting out as a creative is still tough. No matter what you want to create, you'll probably find that hundreds of other people have already had similar ideas. Some of their versions will be worse. Some will be better. The point is, dear reader, that you mustn't get discouraged. In my time as a writer, both online and off, I've learned that two of the most important qualities a person can have as a writer/filmmaker/artist/empanada chef

---

[114] Again, let me express how much caution you should take if you decide to Google any of these. The Power Five were all shock images used to gross out people in the early days of the internet, and while none are traumatic, per se, they're all pretty damn nasty.

are to be *tenacious*, and to be *constantly striving for self-improvement*. Don't be afraid to admit you need to get better—it's something we all have to do.

There are some webcomics and webseries out there that, while they achieve a modest enough success for their creators to make a living doing what they do, they're stagnant. These are creators who put in the work to stick with their project of choice, pumping out update after update filled with words, words, words, but don't have the inner drive to admit that what they're doing isn't perfect. They're lazy; content to wallow in mediocrity rather than buckle down, move past their own egos and improve. Every single person I've listed in this book, no matter what they've done, has had to work their butts off to achieve what they have and improve their skill set. People may enviously begrudge accomplished folks like Chris Hardwick or Felicia Day for their success, but they're not taking into account the tremendous amount of work it took to reach where they are. The unpaid hours of sweat and toil, the time Hardwick and Day undoubtedly spent worrying that they were wasting their lives and praying to the universe that someone else out there gets the message they wanted to put out.

But, because they stuck to their passion and worked to get better, these two are among the hottest names in the geek kingdom. If you're a writer who wants to get your novel published, or an artist who wants people to buy your pictures, or a dude who is crazy about making empanadas and selling them online, learn from their example and *stay the course.* Starting out and sticking with it is the most difficult part, I assure you. Put in the hours, learn to better yourself, and, for God's sake, Niles, ABC: Always Be Creating.

Any creative types who want to learn from example and anyone looking for cool content on the web would do well to check out the folks listed below.

Amazingly Awesome Artists

There are a lot of great artists out there, but these diligent folks not only have the skills to pay the bills, they do so with a distinctly geeky flair.

TRACY J. BUTLER

Best known for: *Lackadaisy,* a webcomic which presents a beautifully illustrated world set in the prohibition era, with anthropomorphic kitty cats dealing with life at the bottom of the economic food chain. If Don Bluth were still around, he'd probably option this in a heartbeat, and hire Tracy as head animator.

GENZOMAN

Best known for: Official *World of Warcraft* art, *Double Dragon Neon.*

KERRY CALLEN

Best known for: Masterfully drawn parody covers of superhero comics that never existed, but should have, like Captain America being forced to eat his shield lest he die, or *The Brave and The Bold* crossover featuring Batman and Jay-Z battling the Riddler. The concepts to Callen's work are all funny, but what really drives the jokes home is how perfectly the artwork and layouts emulate the work of comic book legends like Jack Kirby.

DAVID RAPOZA

Best known for: *Crimson Daggers* and some truly awesome *Teenage Mutant Ninja Turtles, Thundercats, Akira,* and *Super Meat Boy* artwork.

TERRY DODSON

Best known for: Official artwork for issues of *Wonder Woman, Spider-Man, The Defenders,* and *X-Men.*

GEEK
Spotlight

Freddie Wong and Brandon Laatsch

"Stop! Don't do [The Harlem Shake] anymore!"
– Freddie Wong

Sometimes, fame finds all the wrong people. Sometimes, however, it finds all the *right* people. Wong and Laatsch are a writer/director/producer duo whose action-packed Youtube videos quickly gathered fame thanks to their impressive special effects and well-choreographed fight scenes. Some of their most choice clips include a shootout in the old west, an endurance test against a giant metal Crossfire[115] ball, and a gang of CG internet trolls getting massacred. Their webseries, *Video Game High School,* gathered nearly $300,000 dollars on Kickstarter (as well as over 40 million views on Youtube), making it one of the most successful projects Kickstarter had ever helped fund. These two dudes work their butts off to bring the internet fast-paced, funny, and *free* videos, all out of the geeky passion burning in their hearts.

---

[115] CROSSFIRE! You'll get caught up in the ... CROSSFIRE! CROSSFIYAAAAAH!

Websites Which Will Wow Wou

These days, nearly everyone has a blog or a website to call their own. There's a lot of enthusiasm behind them, but their owners often get distracted by real life, or lack the talent and diligence necessary to make their content stand out from the rest. These sites, however, are run by a few bold individuals who have each stepped above and beyond the call of duty to become places people can go to for reliable news and entertainment.

Website: *Ain't It Cool News*
Type of content: Geek news
Who's Behind It: Harry Knowles

After suffering a debilitating accident, Mr. Knowles spent a lot of time on the internet. So much, in fact, that he looked at it and said, "You know what? I wanna play, too." Through the connections he'd made in the various newsgroups and entertainment message boards he was a member of, he gained breaking behind-the-scenes information about everything cool and geeky in Hollywood. From there he continued working, churning out his colorful reviews and getting cutting-edge information, and the site rose to become one of the foremost centers of geeky news.

Website: *Something Awful*
Type of content: Humor, with an emphasis on sarcasm.
Who's Behind It: Rich "Lowtax" Kyanka

Much like Harry Knowles, Lowtax began his website as a mostly personal hobby, but by staking his claim on the internet so early, he, too, unwittingly became the progenitor of something much larger. Something *awful.* The site updates daily with all sorts of original humor articles, the content of which is surprisingly thoughtful given the site's moniker. *SA* is also famous for its message boards, a fascinating place with some of the highest quality message board content you'll find on the internet. The reason? Well, the posters are (generally) smart, passionate folks, and *Something Awful's* moderators are quick to employ the magic ban-hammer on anyone misbehaving, with the site's ten-dollar registration fee helping deter morons from becoming repeat offenders.

Website: *The Mary Sue*
Type of content: Geek news, with a major emphasis on geek girls.
Who's Behind It: Dan Abrams

According to its website, *The Mary Sue* dedicates itself to "highlighting women in the geek world, and providing a prominent place for the voices of geek women. Because all we really want is to be able to geek out with all geeks, of any gender, without feeling as if our femininity is front and center for scrutiny. To not feel like we have to work harder than guys to prove that we're genuinely into geek culture." Essentially, *The Mary Sue* states that geek girls are real, and they wanted a place that was *theirs.* As much as male geeks may claim to be the understanding and inclusive types, countless instances of misogynistic or anti-feminist sentiment has indicated that this, sadly, isn't always the case. *The Mary Sue* works to rectify that with sharply written content that can be enjoyed by everyone and plenty of thoughtful essays and articles about the kind of messages being directed at geek girls.

Website: *Feminist Frequency*

Type of content: Analyses of popular culture

Who's Behind It: Anita Sarkeesian

Another website dedicated to merging feminism and popular culture, *Feminist Frequency* examines movies, television shows, books, and video games through the lens of feminism, breaking down the under-representation of women in entertainment mediums, the *shallowness* with which they (and other minority groups) are often presented, and how important it is that it doesn't continue.[116] If you're a straight, white male, think of it this way—you know Tyler Perry's movies? Whether you're into them or not, you should be glad they're around because they speak to an audience clearly enthusiastic about being spoken to, an audience who *deserves* to have movies that speak to them. Now, imagine that *every* movie was a Tyler Perry movie, except for a few rare exceptions. You'd have *Tyler Perry's Jurassic Park, Tyler Perry's Spider-Man* starring Madea as Aunt May, and *Tyler Perry's Anchorman: The Legend of Rondell Burgundy.* With all of these predominantly African-American movies, don't you think you'd want something that speaks to you? Wouldn't you get tired of having the only characters who represent you be two-dimensional non-people, and wouldn't you also worry about the message being put out there by these caricatures? Not to put words in Ms. Sarkeesian's mouth, but that's one of the points she seems to be making with her pop culture analyses.

Website: *The Other Side of the Story*

Type of content: Tips and tricks for aspiring writers.

Who's Behind It: Janice Hardy, author of *The Shifter* series.

Writing is *tough.* Those of us who write fiction know that we're basically schizophrenics with impressive vocabularies. Like any creative field, it can be difficult to get started as a writer, but

---

[116] Fun fact: in the game *Mega Man X*, the mentor character is Zero, a robot with long, blonde hair that stops below the butt and a rather prominent set of gems across the bust. I played through the game thinking Zero was a girl, but later, after some of the characters finally used a gender-specific pronoun and revealed that she was a he, I found myself disappointed. Zero's still totally badass, but given that there aren't many video game heroes who are women, it was much cooler when I thought he was.

Janice Hardy acts as a big sister to all noobie writers with her easy-to-understand approach to creative mentorship. *The Other Side of the Story* can barely hold all of the writing tips it has, with daily tricks of the trade, analyses of why certain bits of prose may or may not work, and meta-exercises to jolt your writing brain into achieving its full Super Saiyan power.

Website: *Action Flick Chick*

Type of content: Movie news, with an emphasis on science fiction, horror, and, of course, action.

Who's Behind It: Katrina Hill[117]

Let's face it: most movie critics are pretentious, dried up farts. Much like the good folks over at Ain't It Cool News, "Action Flick Chick" Katrina Hill saw this and decided to review movies *her* way, with the kind of humor and personality you can't find anywhere else. She specializes in action movies, though she's been known to review plenty of horror and sci-fi, and she's also quite the convention goer and feminist.

For some other great, geeky websites run by passionate individuals just like you and me, check out: *Gay Gamer, Good to Be a Geek, Shoryuken, NerdSpan, Geekologie, Girl Gone Geek, Awkward Geeks, Nerd Fitness, Topless Robot, The Nerdy Girlie,* and *Blonde Nerd.*

Precocious Podcasts[118]

Radio is pretty much dead. You know it. I know it. Those who work in radio know it, too, they're just holding on for dear life. As with most things, when consumers want radio-esque entertainment nowadays, they turn to the internet. Here you can find music of all sorts, and podcasts, which are like the old radio-interview shows of yesteryear, only the hosts can curse as much as they want since they don't have to answer to the uptight freakin' FCC. There's podcasts about damn near *everything,* especially anything geeky, so I've brought you a few of the more choice podcasts to consider adding to your playlist.

---

[117] Full disclosure: If you've followed my work for a while, you may have noticed the frequent collaborations between myself and Katrina Hill, and that's because we're married. I realize it may seem a little nepotistic to list my wife in this book, but 1. I'm proud of her, and 2. If you had the chance, why wouldn't you brag about your friends and loved ones?

[118] Did you know that "podcast" is derived from combining the words "broadcast" and "iPod?" Why didn't anyone ever tell me? Ted, you've really dropped the ball on this one.

SMODCAST

Category: Comedy

Who's Behind It: Kevin Smith and Scott Mosier

What Is It: Kevin Smith's Smodcast isn't so much a podcast as it is a network. Silent Bob himself, Kevin Smith, was an early adopter of the podcast format, and thanks to his auspicious timing, surprisingly diligent work ethic, and obsession with jokes involving the swimsuit region, he's got an entire series of different hit shows. Under the Smodcast banner you'll find quality programs like *Hollywood Babble-On,* where Ralph Garman and Kev make fun of Hollywood/pop culture, and do so with a deliciously R-rated flair. There's also *Jay and Silent Bob Get Old,* where the dank-namic duo discusses any and everything, as well as dozens of other balls-out shows.

STARTALK

Category: Science

Who's Behind It: Neil Degrasse Tyson

What Is It: Once Astrophysicist Neil Degrasse Tyson stepped out into the internet, he quickly became an icon thanks to his intellect, his wit, and his ability to convey complex topics with both clarity and zeal.[119] In StarTalk, he and his distinguished guests discuss everything from the Big Bang to the science behind a zombie apocalypse.

NIGHT VALE

Category: Meta/horror

Who's Behind It: Written by Joseph Fink and Jeffrey Cranor, and narration provided by Cecil "No relation to Alec" Baldwin.

What Is It: "Community updates" about Night Vale, a fictional *Twilight Zone*-esque small town. What's especially great about this podcast is the calm, matter-of-fact way Cecil describes things like missing persons and skulking, hooded figures.

TALKIN' TOONS

Category: Animation/show business

Who's Behind It: Voice acting legend Rob Paulsen, who you may know as Raphael from the '80s *Ninja Turtles* cartoon, Donatello from the 2013 *Ninja Turtles* cartoon, Pinky from *Pinky & The Brain,* Yakko from *Animaniacs*, and about a billion other roles.

What Is It: Rob Paulsen sits down with some of his voice acting cohorts to discuss the business of acting with your vocal cords. Voice actors are some of the most talented performers in

---

[119] He's also famous for being the reference for the "Watch Out, We've Got a Badass Over Here" meme.

Hollywood, and yet, because they do their jobs mostly off-camera, they're not as recognized as their on-camera counterparts. Rob talks with other legends such as Phil LaMarr, Billy West, John DiMaggio, Jennifer Hale, Maurice LaMarche, Steve Blum, Nolan North, Tara Strong, Cree Summer, and Grey Delisle, just to name a few. In addition to providing interesting stories about helping create some of the most iconic animated characters in history, Rob and his guests have funny, fast-paced conversations that make for remarkably smooth listening—they are *voice actors*, after all.

WRITING EXCUSES

Category: Writing

Who's Behind It: Mary Robinette Kowal, Brandon Sanderson, Howard Tayler, and Dan Wells.

What Is It: Writing Excuses helps writers of any age or experience level get into the writing mindset by providing helpful examples from both the lives of the podcasters themselves and from popular culture.

YOGSCAST

Category: Gaming/comedy/general sweetness

Who's Behind It: Lewis Brindley, Simon Lane, and a butt-ton of other talented folks.

What Is It: According to the Yogscast website, Yogscast "Originally formed in 2008 as a way for Lewis to share Simon with the world, The Yogscast started off life providing some of the most respected *World of Warcraft* boss guides to-date. In early 2009, the duo founded the #1 ranked podcast, the YoGPoD." This goofball duo-turned-internet media powerhouse formed out of the shadow of Ye Olde Goon Squad, a *World of Warcraft* guild based out of the *Something Awful* forums, and quickly took off thanks to their sharp content and marvelously entertaining Youtube videos guiding users through the wondrous world of indie gaming masterpiece *Minecraft*.

THE INSTANCE

Category: Gaming

Who's Behind It: Scott Johnson and company.

What Is It: A weekly podcast devoted to everyone's favorite money-sucking, soul-destroying, fantastically fun lootfest, *World of Warcraft*.

GEEK Spotlight

Felicia Day

"You can craft who you want to be online in a way which is unique, and that's amazing."

Actress, writer, and ex-video game addict Felicia Day has made quite the name for herself in the geek world. She's most famous for her work on *The Guild,* as well as starring in the cult musical *Dr. Horrible's Sing-Along Blog.* Day's smart as a whip. No, she's way smarter than a whip—whips are idiots. She graduated as valedictorian and, in college, double majored in mathematics and music performance. Nowadays you can find her in a zillion great guest spots on shows such as *Supernatural* and *Eureka,* as well as all over her Youtube channel, *Geek and Sundry.* Day is a testament to all hopeful geeks who just want to do what they love—if you stick with it and put in the work, your awesomeness will shine through.

NERDIST

Category: Comedy/General Nerdery

Who's Behind It: Chris Hardwick, with Matt Mira and Jonah Ray.

What Is It: Comedian Chris Hardwick teams up with all sorts of geeks, show-biz legends, and comedy gurus to discuss all sorts of great stuff, like Tom Hanks' love of antique typewriters, Joel McHale's son dressing up as a light switch for Halloween, and Conan O'Brien's approach to comedy/having amazing hair.

Tumblrs and Tweeters

Tumblr and Twitter are minimalist communication sites. With Twitter's character limit and the Tumblr userbase's propensity toward explaining themselves in .gif form, neither site provides the best venue for in-depth analyses or thoughtful conversations. But what they do excel at, however, is *weirdness*. There are numerous Tumblrs and Twitters dedicated to bizarre concepts. Some are funny. Most are just strange.[120]

GEEK
Spotlight

Chris Hardwick

"No human ever became interesting by not failing. The more you fail and recover and improve, the better you are as a person. Ever meet someone who's always had everything work out for them with zero struggle? They usually have the depth of a puddle. Or they don't exist."

Chris Hardwick might as well be called Chris Hardwork,[121] because this guy has worked his butt off to get where he is. This comedian/musician/nerdist extraordinaire knows what he loves, and he pours 100% of himself into his work. His Nerdist podcast boomed into a multimedia empire thanks to Hardwick's tireless dedication to providing consistent content, his affable sense of humor, and the many awesome people he's teamed up with. Anyone looking to forge their own way creatively would do well to take notes from the way Hardwick approaches things so humanely; if you want to be successful in the geek world, don't be a wangchung about stuff.

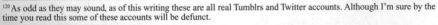

---

[120] As odd as they may sound, as of this writing these are all real Tumblrs and Twitter accounts. Although I'm sure by the time you read this some of these accounts will be defunct.

[121] Bad-ump TISH!

Tumblr: The Same Picture of Dave Coulier Every Day

Content: Can you guess? That's right—every single day this Tumblr's owner posts the same picture of Dave Coulier. It's a nice pic of ol' Uncle Joey, to be sure, but the question remains: how long can this madness continue?

Tumblr: Selleck Waterfall Sandwich

Content: A variety of pictures that all contain the same three elements: actor Tom Selleck, a waterfall, and a sandwich.

Tumblr: Ugly Renaissance Babies

Content: During the Renaissance, rather than track down infants to use as reference when painting pictures *containing* infants, many artists would simply paint small adults because it was easier. The result is there are a lot of really ugly-looking Renaissance babies out there.

Tumblr: Ok, Weirdo

Content: Messages, screen caps, and pictures of people behaving like total freaking nutjobs on the dating site Okcupid.com.

Tumblr: Disney's Newest Character, Nigel Thornberry

Content: A collection of photoshopped images wherein Disney characters have been replaced by that homely wildlife lover, Nigel Thornberry.[122]

Tumblr: Memos From Fury

Content: Running S.H.I.E.L.D. can be a tough job, especially when you factor in having to babysit a bunch of superpowered goofballs who keep doing things such as confusing Captain America by showing him *Inglorious Basterds* and trying to convince him that's how World War II *really* ended, or stealing the S.H.I.E.L.D. stationery and replacing it with notepads covered in Lisa Frank-esque pink hearts.

Tumblr: Sims Gone Wrong

Content: The Sims may be a fun people simulator, but it's also prone to glitching out in horrifying ways, like naked parents casually putting on a hand puppet show for a child's birthday party, or firefighters deciding not to fight a fire and instead gently play their guitar, or the Grim Reaper dying and having to collect his own soul.

---

[122] To be clear, Nigel is homely and loves wildlife; as far as anyone knows, he doesn't love homely wildlife.

Twitter: Not a cop

Content: This twitter account does *not* belong to a cop. He's just a cool guy who wants to party with the druggies. He's lost the number to his drug dealer, though, so you'll have to help him by giving him the number to yours. His hobbies include drugs and crime—let him know if you're doing either so he can join you.

Twitter: KimKierkegaardashian

Content: As described by its author, Kim Kierkegaardashian merges the philosophy of Søren Kierkegaard with the vapid tweets of Kim Kardashian. It's a hilarious, often dark, look at the hollow consumerism and celebrity worship that haunts modern life.

Twitter: Bill Nye Tho

Content: Espouses weed-infused, grammatically blasphemous tidbits about science as if they were from a Bill Nye from a parallel universe, one where he's high all the time. Some his scientific ponderances include: "RT IF U STILL AWAKE THINKIN ABOUT WATER VAPOR IN DA ATMOSPHERE OF MARS" and "if u dont go apeshit thinkin bout all the volcanoes in the ocean then gtfo my face." Wise words, Bill Nye Tho.

Twitter: Drunk Hulk

Content: When the Incredible Hulk gets a hold of liquor strong enough to affect his system, the results aren't pretty, and are often in all-caps.

Twitter: Coffee Dad

Content: Mostly tweets about coffee, but occasionally tweets remorse over his fictional dead son.

Twitter: Two Bros

Content: A slew of tweets about the kinds of activities two bros might enjoy; things such as: "Two bros thinkin bout chimichangas tonight." "Two bros enjoying a sunset." "Two bros hugging it out after a lengthy dispute."

Twitter: The Dark Lord

Content: Did you know Voldemort has a twitter? He does, though he mostly uses it to bitch about muggles and that Potter kid.

Twitter: Big Ben Clock

Content: Every hour, on the hour, this twitter account tweets a number of BONG onomatopoeias to match what time it is.

Twitter: Horse E-Books

Content: Spams Twitter with random excerpts from horse-related books. Choice tweets include: "How to Teach a Horse to Sit, Give a Kiss and Give a Hug"; "Unfortunately, as you probably know, people"; "Their negativity only served to push me deeper into the realm of soap-making."

Wascally Webcomics

Many fine webcomics grace the digital halls of the internet. There are also many crappy ones stinking up the place, vanity projects which the creator quickly forgot about after a few weeks of updates. If you want to familiarize yourself with some great comics who help *expand* the medium instead of just taking up more space, why not check out the following:[123]

Title: *Paranatural*
Who's Behind It: Zach Morrison[124]
Why It's So Great: Morrison's creative skills are impressive, to say the least, given that he not only created the unique, ghost-filled world of *Paranatural,* but that he populates it with living characters so dripping with personality it'll make you more interesting just by reading them. And his art is both kinetic and expressive.

Title: *Magical Game Time*
Who's Behind It: Zach Gorman
Why It's So Great: Zach Gorman manages to succinctly summarize the emotional content of a video game—what it felt like playing it—and reflect it thoughtfully with his creative art and penchant for wistfulness.

---

[123] For more webcomic suggestions, check out the webcomic section of *The Geek Handbook*, also written by yours truly. I feature several other prominent comics, like *Penny Arcade* and *PVP*, there, which is why I didn't write about them here.
[124] Not to be confused with Zach Morris, the blonde-haired protagonist of *Saved by The Bell*, or Evil Zach Morris, the black-haired protagonist of *Damned by the Bell*.

Title: *Penultimate Quest*

Who's Behind It: Lars Brown

Why It's So Great: While initially it seems that Penultimate Quest is simply a comic book tale of characters living their lives like video game characters, underneath the surface it's a thoughtful examination of the repetition of our daily lives ... and a kick-ass monster-slaying adventure with some great visual flair and funny dialogue.

Title: *Whomp!*

Who's Behind It: Ronnie Filyaw

Why It's So Great: While most webcomic artists seek to glorify themselves with idealized, Mary Sue self-inserts, Ronnie Filyaw throws himself on the comedy grenade and does the exact opposite. This tri-weekly webcomic tells the tale of lonely, Chicken McNugget and anime-obsessed comic artist Ronnie, his surprisingly normal roommate Agrias, and Motivation Dude, who is basically the world's most aggressive muse.

Title: *The Non-Adventures of Wonderella*

Who's Behind It: Justin Pierce

Why It's So Great: Pierce's playful take on traditional superheroes manages to be funny, modern, and, when the moment is right, delightfully crass.

Title: *Plume*

Who's Behind It: K. Lynn Smith

Why It's So Great: This fantasy tale about revenge in the old west incorporates smart world-building with a kickass hero and gorgeous, stylish art.

Title: *Dr. McNinja*

Who's Behind It: Christopher Hastings (Writer/Artist), Anthony Clark (Colorist)

Why It's So Great: A ninja doctor punches T-rexes, robots, and Draculas. If there are better things in life than that, I don't want to know about them because I don't think I could handle it.

If you're a fan of webcomics, consider also checking out: *Dresden Codak, Unsounded, Hinges, Derelict, Monster of the Week,* and *Octopus Pie.*

The Shape of the Internet: Meme, Myself, and I

Have you ever stopped to consider the shape of the internet? I don't mean it's condition, I mean it's geometric, metaphysical shape. In its early years the internet was mostly straight lines— zipping bits of communication heading directly from one source to another with things such as e-mail and instant messaging. But as it progressed it grew arms, tendrils, even; when message boards became big information wasn't a one-to-one experience, it was one-to-infinity. Things grew louder and rounder, with more and more people discovering the wonders of the World Wide Web and contending to make their voices heard. Now it's an amorphous din that's both wonderful and occasionally overwhelming, with everyone fighting to get themselves and their opinions out there, banding together based around entirely new sets of ideas that exist solely on the internet.

And that's where memes come in.

Five of the Most Unpopular Memes of All Time

5 | Entomology Enthusiast Esmerelda

What it's about: jokes that only bug collectors of Romani descent would understand.

4 | Fresh-water Frederico

What it's about: various kinds of equipment used by fresh-water fisherman, and the ongoing enmity they feel towards deep-sea fishermen.

3 | The Overworked Orangutan

What it's about: an orangutan whose kids don't appreciate her, and whose place in the hierarchy of her ape clan is constantly threatened.

2 | Disco Dartmouth Dan

What it's about: cultural movements, events, and locations that were popular on the Dartmouth College campus in the 1970s.

1 | The Knee

What it's about: what your right knee thinks about on a day-to-day basis.

Evolutionary biologist Richard Dawkins coined the term to describe the spread of information. Currently most denizens of the 'net merely think of memes as pictures of animals with multi-colored backgrounds behind them and impact font surrounding them. Internet memes are quick, easy, infrequently funny ways for people to get a message out there, whether that message is about qualities an ideal dating partner should have, the quirky habits we all have, or the many things which might incite survivalist Bear Grylls to drink his own urine.

The Top Ten Most Unpopular #Hashtags

10 | #ThingsMyButtToldMe

9 | #MakinPlaydohAtThaClub

8 | #GonnaFreakOutIfIDon'tGetSomeDangGoldenGrahamsLikeRightNow

7 | #AnOstrichADayKeepsJackHannahAway

6 | #DiarreahIsForWinners

5 | #TooManyLemursTooLittleTime

4 | #DamnUStank

3 | #DamnIStank

2 | #MakingResponsibleDecisions

1 | #BringBackPoochinski

Social Media, or Why You Shouldn't Tweet About Your Poop

It's wonderful that information technology has advanced so prolifically that, at any given time, you can find almost any bit of information you could ever need. The flip-side to that never-ending stream of data, however, is that you have to filter through much inanity. I'm talking about tweets, likes, and status updates, people. Two basic facts about people: (1) A person's favorite topic tends to be his or herself. (2) Most people's favorite topic is really freaking boring. That inner banality doesn't them from instagramming pictures of themselves eating at the same restaurant for five meals in a row, or talking about how they wish they had more money. We all eat, we all need money. Perhaps we should make an effort to make the world a more interesting place by filtering out the hum-drum crap. Just because a #hashtag is popular doesn't mean that its respective contents are worth tweeting about. Of course, just because a #hashtag is *unpopular* doesn't mean it should be ignored.

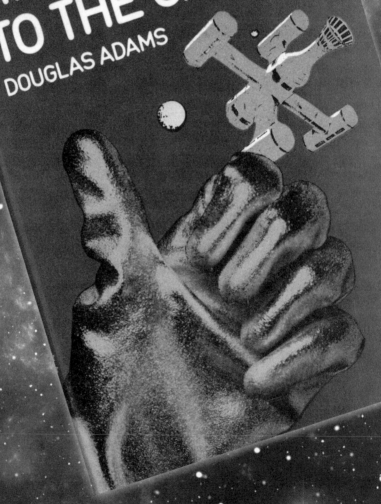

Chapter 6

Take a Look, It's in a Book

In this era of smart phones, tablets, and pervasive internet connectivity, books still play a vital role in our culture because of their ability to cheaply tell an in-depth story. Oddly enough, in much the same way that television shows often get consumed on something *other* than a television, the modern book is about as likely to be read on an iPad as it is on paper. Both traditional novels and graphic novels are high investment, high reward types of entertainment. It may take you longer to get through a good book than it would a movie, but isn't that kind of the point? Part of the beauty of a novel is that the better your imagination is, the better your story becomes, rewarding readers who are quick-thinking and creative.

Horror movies may scare you, but once they shine the light on the monster at the end of the movie, the fear begins to wane; we've seen the beast, and now we know what it is. As human beings, we're the apex predators of planet Earth—the biggest and baddest mofos around. There's not a thing out there we can't fight, or, at bare minimum, *try* to fight. But while a horror movie is limited by the very real fact that humans are the top dogs, a horror novel is unfettered by such restraints. If the book you're reading is about a monster that's the scariest thing you can imagine, you're going to envision the *scariest thing you can imagine.*

Similarly, if you are unimpressed by HBO's depiction of King's Landing, or don't think the *Going Postal* TV movie quite nailed the look of the Patrician's office, it's because your imagination is the greatest special effect around. Technology becomes outdated, special effects wither and become comical with time, but the power of a good book is eternal.

It's why classics such as J.R.R Tolkien's *The Lord of the Rings* still work decades after their initial publications. That, and the fact that we call such books *classics* for a reason. Many consider Tolkien the progenitor of the modern fantasy genre—he *was* the first author to feature such fantasy staples as

elves, dwarves, and pointy wizard hats.

A bit of warning, however, is that, should you attempt to read any of Tolkien's works nowadays, you may find them a bit on the chewy side. When compared to the tightly edited books of today, Tolkien's epic fantasies can seem somewhat meandering and overly detailed.[125]

For some other classic fantasy novels that have some charming old-timey roughness around their edges, check out: L. Frank Baum's *The Wizard of Oz* series, which is comprised of a whopping thirty plus books, Lewis Carrol's *Alice in Wonderland* and *Through the Looking Glass*, the many works of Roald Dahl, the *A Wizard of Earthsea* series by Ursula K. Le Guin, and *The Chronicles of Narnia* series by C.S. Lewis.

---

[125] Although meandering and excess detail are pretty common features to fantasy stories, so if you're a fan of the genre it may not bother you.

Classic Science Fiction and Horror:
I Have No Eyes But I Must Read

While Tolkien spent many years acting as bit of a single dad to fantasy, science fiction has always had an extended family to draw from. Jules Verne, H.G. Wells, and Mary Shelley are three of the earliest names to help shape the genre. Verne penned such classics as *Twenty Thousand Leagues Under the Sea, Around the World in Eighty Days,* and *Sixty-Seven Smackdowns in Space.*[126] His novels often contained oddly prophetic uses of technology that, while extraordinary in the era they were written, ended up becoming commonplace. He also influenced great minds such as cosmonaut Yuri Gagarin, explorer/scientists Fridjof Nansen, the Father of Rocket Science Wernher Von Braun, and aeronaut Alberto Santos-Dumont, as well as writers Ray Bradbury, J.R.R. Tolkien, and Jean Cocteau.

H.G. Wells, otherwise known as Herbert George Wells, Helena G. Wells, and H-Dizzle-Well-U-Know, had a knack for the fantastic (unlike most other writers of his era). He also had a penchant for beginning the title of his novels with the word "The." *The Time Machine* is the first story to feature a machine to allow deliberate travel through time. *The Island of Doctor Moreau* dealt heavily in human responsibility, morality, and primitive "gene splicing" via vivisection. *The Invisible Man* was about a dude who turned invisible and got carried away with naked, utterly disinhibited shenanigans. *The War of the Worlds* told the story of a Martian invasion of Earth, and how even the mightiest of foes can be toppled with something seemingly insignificant. In this case, it was bacteria, but it was also a metaphor for human bravery, colonialism, social Darwinism, and for individuals standing against seemingly impossible odds (a theme that was quite popular circa World War II).

If Verne and Wells were science fiction's fathers and/or cool uncles, then Mary Shelley was its awesome aunt. She wrote many pieces of literature throughout her life, though none ever drew the universal acclaim and importance of *Frankenstein*. Most consider this to be the first piece of true science fiction ever written, as well as being a key piece of literature in the propagation of horror as a genre.

Search even just a bit and you'll find countless retellings of *Frankenstein*. There's Universal Studio's 1931 classic *Frankenstein*, which is perhaps the most well-known imagining of the horror tale. There's also Kenneth

---

[126] All right, so I made that last one up.

THE WAR OF THE WORLDS

H. G. WELLS

LOOKING GLASS LIBRARY

PRICE SIXPENCE

FRANKENSTEIN
BY Mrs. SHELLEY.

ROUTLEDGE AND SONS

Branagh's *Mary Shelley's Frankenstein,* a flick that takes some serious liberties with the source materials (which is especially ironic given the name), and a number of other *Frankenstein*-related projects, the quality of which varies wildly. Eventually the tale of *Frankenstein* became so well-known it was robbed of all horror, during which time filmmakers capitalized on its open license to create all sorts of Frankenstein parodies. Among the more well-known titles is *Young Frankenstein*, the classic comedy from legendary funnyman Mel Brooks, as well as some not-so-good entries, like *Frankenhooker*, which is about a reanimated prostitute, and *Blackenstein*, which is about—you guessed it—a reanimated black guy. If things continue down this path, I shudder to think what sort of Frankenstein parodies we'll see.

The Top Five Worst Frankenstein Parodies Possibly In Development

5 | *Dankenstein.*
A monster made from patched-together corpses gets brought to life and sits around smoking weed every day.

4 | *Stankenstein.*
A monster made from patched-together corpses gets brought to life and refuses to bathe himself.

3 | *Bankenstein.*
A monster made from patched-together corpses gets brought to life and opens a small-town bank.

2 | *Prankenstein.*
A monster made from patched-together corpses gets brought to life and commits his life to pulling practical jokes on any and everyone.

1 | *Hankenstein.*
A monster made from patched-together corpses gets brought to life and goes on to sell propane and propane accessories.

Speaking of horror, one of the biggest names to hit the horror-sphere of American literature is, without a doubt, Stephen King. The man's gift for crafting dark prose is unparalleled, and his stories contain moment after moment that will forever be seared into the deepest, darkest corners of his audiences' memory banks. Some of King's most notable works include *Misery*, a tale of an injured author being cared for[127] by his most enthusiastic fan[128] who drives him home[129] once he's recovered. His popular *Dark Tower* series took over twenty years to reach completion, so if you're in the mood for an epic, genre-spanning work look no further. *The Shining* is a seminal piece of horror about the horrors of hotel management. There's also *Carrie, Salem's Lot, The Stand, Christine,* and many, many others. Oh, and *of course, It.* Several of King's works have been adapted into other forms of media, and while the film version of *The Shining* may be the most famous adaptation of King's novels, it's *It*, starring Tim "Sweet Transvestite" Curry, that most younger fans remember for Curry's coulrophobia[130]-inducing performance as Pennywise the Clown. While the movie's finale doesn't hold up well when compared to modern special effects, Pennywise the Clown is something straight out of your worst nightmares. Plus, when adapting *It* from page to screen, the filmmakers made the wise choice of leaving a few things out—namely, the under-aged gang bang which takes place between seven boys and a lone girl, all twelve years old, as a way of them making an oath of secrecy.[131]

---

[127] Held hostage.

[128] Stalker.

[129] Chops off his foot with an axe and cauterizes the wound with a blowtorch.

[130] Coulrophobia: the fear of clowns.

[131] Seriously, Stephen King, what the French toast? There's being creepy like classic horror, and being creepy like that one dude who lives down the hall and only ever wears a bathrobe, and that scene was definitely the latter.

First Hand Geekiness: Edgar Allen Poe

If you want to find the beginnings of speculative fiction (that special geeky triumvirate of fantasy, science fiction, and horror) in American literature, look no further than Edgar Allan Poe. The fact that one of the greats, Mr. Ray Bradbury himself, called him "My Papa" shows the imprint Poe has stamped on the hearts of book geeks everywhere. Most know Poe as master of the macabre—sending horror and dark fantasy booming onto the romanticism scene—but he was also fundamental in the development of the science fiction genre as we know it, influencing such giants as Jules Verne. Even fewer folks are aware that Poe almost single-handedly created the detective story, which of course influenced Sir Arthur Conan Doyle, the creator of Sherlock Holmes, which later inspired characters ranging from Nancy Drew to Dr. Gregory House. But Poe was more than even that; he was also a poet, a literary critic, and one of the first artists in America to attempt to make a living off of writing alone—the beginning of the creative professional of today. Much is said about Poe as a man. Dozens, if not hundreds, of biographies have tried to illuminate the dark mysteries of his life, but in my opinion, not enough is said about the legacy of his work. He was and still is, quite simply, the best of the best. His footsteps will forever echo down the corridors of the literary canon.

– Annie Neugebauer
Short story author, novelist, poet
www.annieneugebauer.com

If you dare to check out the umbrous works of more classic horror authors, steel your nerves and seek out: *H.P. Lovecraft, August Derleth,*[132] *Clive Barker, Richard Matheson,* and *Algernon Blackwood.*

Modern Fantasy and Science Fiction: Parody With a Side of Self-Awareness

To simply refer to the writings of Terry Pratchett as humor does both him and yourself a broad disservice. Stories set within his *Discworld* typically contain comedic elements parodying fantasy tropes, but they also contain some of the most fleshed-out characters, locations, and stories you'll ever see. Pratchett has a knack for capturing voices, and for coming at a subject from an angle so unknown and so brilliant that you'll smack yourself in the head and say, "Of course!" His novels feature many different protagonists, but a few of the most popular recurring characters include Samuel Vimes, commander of the Ankh-Morpork city watch and an ambivalent idealist/cynic with hard fists and an even harder head. There's also Rincewind, an unaccomplished, haggard wizard often compared by his contemporaries as "the magical equivalent to the number zero." Adventure constantly seeks out Rincewind, and he constantly tries to tell it that he's out sick. He's a coward adept at cowardice, and a wizard who only knows one spell—a bit of arcana so powerful it scares all other magic out of his head if he tries to learn any. In the more rural parts of the Disc, you'll find a witchy trio composed of the stubborn and unstoppable Granny Weatherwax, the jolly and dirty-minded Nanny Ogg, and several apprentice witches who join their coven before moving on. You've also got Death, who SPEAKS IN SMALL CAPS AND IS QUITE FOND OF CURRY, Moist Von Lipwig, who could con the pants off of Donald Duck, and Tiffany Aching, an accomplished young witch prone to meta-thought exercises.

Honestly, there are so many great Discworld protagonists, antagonists, and side characters, it would almost be folly to list them for the uninitiated.

Almost.

---

[132] While Lovecraft is credited as the creator of the Cthulhu mythos, which is oh-so popular today, Derleth contributed a significant chunk of work towards it, too. He's just not as well-known as Lovecraft.

Eleven of *Discworld's* Greatest Side Characters

11 | **Foul Ole Ron**

Occupation: Beggar

First Introduced: *Feet of Clay*

Note: Known for a Smell so strong it deserves capitalization, and has evolved a personality of its own. Ron's Smell has a taste for high society and often visits art galleries and opera houses.

10 | **Evil-Minded Son of a Bitch**

Occupation: Camel

First Introduced: *Moving Pictures*

Note: Like most camels, Evil-Minded Son of a Bitch is too intelligent to admit to his intelligence.

9 | **Wallace Sonky**

Occupation: Owner, inventor, and chief proprietor of *Sonky's Rubber Goods*

First Introduced: *The Fifth Elephant*

Note: Though his death is untimely, Sonky's contributions to Ankh-Morpork will never be forgotten, because without him (and, more importantly, his prophylactic invention), the city's housing problems would have been even more pressing.

8 | **Leonard of Quirm**

Occupation: Inventor

First Introduced: *Wyrd Sisters*

Note: Like his real-life counterpart, Leonardo da Vinci, Leonard is a brilliant inventor whose blueprints include inventions for flying, exploration, and wartime. He considers his martial inventions mere exercises, as he doesn't think anyone would ever be mad enough to use them.

7 | **Mustrum Ridcully**

Occupation: Archchancellor of the Unseen University

First Introduced: *Moving Pictures*

Note: Does a lot for rare species of animals—mostly by keeping them rare.

6 | The Quite Reverend Mightily-Praiseworth-Are-Ye-Who-Exalteth Om Oats

Occupation: Reverend

First Introduced: *Carpe Jugulum*

Note: At a church-sanctioned child-naming event, he accidentally named the child "Esmerelda Margaret Note Spelling" due to his own nervousness.

5 | Hodgesaargh

Occupation: Lancre Falconer

First Introduced: *Lords and Ladies*

Note: Author of *The Arts of Falconrie and Hawking.* Hodgesaargh spends most of his days training/getting mauled by his birds, hence his unusual moniker.

4 | Bloody Stupid Johnson

Occupation: Gardener/Inventor

First Introduced: Though he is dead by the time the first *Discworld* book is set, his idiotic inventions live on after him.

Note: Infamous for being unable to invent anything according to any semblance of common sense. It's suggested that he possessed "inverse genius," meaning that he was as far from incompetent as a true genius is, but it was impossible for a layman to tell the difference at a glance.

3 | The Librarian

Occupation: Librarian/orangutan

First Introduced: *The Colour of Magic*

Note: Never, under any circumstances, should you refer to this wizard-turned-noble-ape as a monkey.

2 | Cut-Me-Own-Throat Dibbler

Occupation: Salesman

First Introduced: *Guards! Guards!*

Note: His sausages-inna-bun are so repulsive they'll make you never want to eat again, but his sales acumen is so sharp you'll probably find yourself buying a second one.

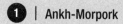 | **Ankh-Morpork**

Occupation: City

First Introduced: *The Colour of Magic*

Note: Also known as the Big Wahooni, this city is so well-defined it's a character unto itself; you know how it (and its inhabitants) will react to anything, be it panicking over dragons, watching impassive as the Clown's Guild joylessly goofs around while trying to prevent their guild hall from burning, or getting swept up in the latest craze of postage stamps.

If you want your fantasy novels with a twinge of humor, also check out: the *MythAdventures* series by Robert Lynn Asprin and Jody Lynn Nye, the *Majyk* series by Esther Friesner, the *Xanth* series by Piers Anthony, pretty much anything by Tom Holt, and the *Magic Kingdom of Landover* series by Terry Brooks.

Of course, no discussion of fantasy literature would be complete without mentioning the box-office murdering, horcrux-destroying, multimedia juggernaut that is the *Harry Potter* series. Love it or hate it, this wizarding franchise made both fantasy and reading cool again, and encouraged millions of kids to hit the books.

Everyone knows what *Harry Potter* is about ... wait, hold on. You in the back, yes, I see you raising your hand.

Mmm-hmm. Really?

You've never even *heard* of Harry Potter? I find that hard to believe. Don't get offended. I'm not calling you a liar, I'm just saying it's improbable ... that you're not lying.

Fine. For the *one* person in the back who was apparently in a coma for the last decade and a half, the *Harry Potter* series centers around a young boy of the same name who one day finds out that he's a wizard. Suddenly he's swept over to a magical school filled with dire secrets, arcane dangers, and a BFF or two. Since Harry primarily exists to move the plot along and provide a nascent viewpoint for the audience, he, himself, isn't that interesting of a character. The many, many characters around him, however, are the real heart of *Harry Potter*. Folks like Ron Weasley, Albus Dumbledore, Luna Lovegood, and, of course, Hermione Granger.

Geeky Influences: *Harry Potter*

Harry Potter **got kids to read.** For years, parents and teachers have fought with their kids to get them to discover the wonderful world of books—LeVar Burton's *Reading Rainbow* helped, but he's only one man. It took a media-cultural force of epic proportions to start dragging kids away from television screens and back into bookstores, and that force was named *Harry Flipping Potter*. The books' widespread success lead to youths everywhere suddenly doing what they'd previously considered unthinkable and picking up a book. *Harry Potter* made reading cool

Hermione Granger

"You know, the Egyptians used to worship cats."

Hermione Granger: professionally precocious genius. Without Hermione around, two things are clear: Harry would have died halfway through *The Chamber of Secrets,* and Ron would've lost his virginity to Hannah Abbott, which would have left poor Nevile Longbottom in the cold. Sure, Hermione may be a know-it-all to the point of frequent obnoxiousness, but she's incredibly moral (sometimes inflexibly so) and the reason she's such a know-it-all is because she pretty much *does* know it all. J.K. Rowling herself stated the clinical usefulness of Hermione, in that, because of her ridiculously encyclopedic knowledge, it was never out of character for her to know some useful bit of exposition.

again, and once kids finished reading *Potter*, they looked around to see what other novels might catch their fancy.

It fostered creativity. Not only did *Potter* get kids to read, it got them to write, to draw, to *do*. Nascent writers took to the keyboards to pound out fan fiction starring their favorite imagined *Potter* pairings, like Draco and Hermione, or Hagrid and Dobby.[133] Young artists cut their teeth on pictures of the boy who lived and his many companions. Hell, it even inspired some creative fashion in the sartorially minded community, with some trying on scarves and long coats for the first time, and knitters making scarves that rocked their favorite house colors.

Another young adult literary powerhouse, *The Hunger Games*, focuses far more on dystopic darkness than spells and goblins. At base, *The Hunger Games* mixes the horrors of war with the faux-human elements of reality shows. It also gave us one hell of a kickass heroine: Katniss Everdeen.

First-Hand Geekiness: Katniss Everdeen

"Katniss Everdeen—the girl on fire! Katniss, heroine of the book and film series *The Hunger Games*, is by far one of the best heroines pop culture has ever seen, right up there next to Ripley and Sarah Connor. We first meet Katniss when she's on the hunt, breaking the law and putting herself potentially in harm's way in order to provide for her family. Immediately we see not only her bravery, but her diligence as a hunter and skill with a bow. Despite being only sixteen, she's a strong, independent lady who'll do anything to take care of her sister Prim—which we see again when she volunteers for the brutal Hunger Games in Prim's stead. Katniss shows the kind of proactive bravery that few protagonists, particularly *female* protagonists, ever do.

Throughout the rest of the story her reputation as a heroine never becomes undermined. Too often in films a "heroine" will be made weak at some point and have to either be saved by her (often male) partner, or rely on what are considered typically feminine qualities, like compassion and empathy, to come out victorious. In *The Hunger Games,* Katniss is the one doing the saving and her male partner, Peeta, is the soft-hearted, compassionate one. *The Hunger Games*' antagonist, President Snow, sees her as his biggest threat—not Peeta, nor any of the other victors.

As a female pop culture consumer, it's frustrating to see so many "heroines"

---

[133] You think I'm kidding about the Hagrid X Dobby stuff. I'm not. Don't Google it if you value your sanity.

relegated to passive roles, not actually contributing anything while their male protectors do all the work (*Twilight*). Katniss, as we see her in *The Hunger Games*, is the architect of her own destiny. She volunteers to save her sister, she chooses to defy the gamemakers during the Games, and she sets an example for both women and people in general on how to defy gender roles and be an active part in deciding who to be and how to live."

– Katrina Hill
Author of *Action Movie Freak*
@actionchick

Douglas Adams' *Hitchhiker's Guide to the Galaxy* trilogy is comprised of the following books: *The Hitchhiker's Guide to the Galaxy; The Restaurant at the End of the Universe; Life, the Universe, and Everything; So Long and Thanks for All the Fish;* and *Mostly Harmless*. Yes, if you were counting, that's five books. There've also been radio plays, television specials, a movie or two, and a sort-of-official sequel penned by the devilishly clever Eoin Colfer. Thanks to Adams' rapier wit and thoughtful subversion of sci-fi tropes, this strange, manic, and occasionally frantic, multimedia monster has forever left its searing brand on the hide of popular culture. Neil Gaiman, friend and fan of Adams, said of the author that "He was unique and absolutely irreplaceable and incredibly kind." Adams may have headed off to the restaurant at the end of the universe far too soon, but his legacy will continue to inspire those around him until long after the Ravenous Bugblatter Beast of Traal has consumed the last Vogon's grandmother.

For more great fantasy and sci-fi fiction, check out: *The Dresden Files* by Jim Butcher, *Ender's Game* by Orson Scott Card, the *Shannara* series by Terry Brooks, *American Gods* by Neil Gaiman, the *Game of Thrones (A Song of Ice and Fire)* series by George R.R. Martin[134], *Dune* by Frank Herbert, *Fahrenheit 451* by Ray Bradbury, *Do Androids Dream of Electric Sheep* by Philip K. Dick, *The Wheel of Time* series by Robert Jordan, the *Belgariad* series by David Eddings, *The Princess Bride* by William Goldman, *The Kingkiller Chronicles* by Patrick Rothfuss, and *Neuromancer* by William Gibson.

Comic Books and Graphic Novels

Superheroes: The Birth of Comic Books as We Know Them

It might be weird to think it, but there was an era when superheroes, as we know them, didn't exist. This was roughly around the same era that we lived in filthy pits and flung our poo at each other—otherwise known as the Age of Pits and Poo.[135] Superheroes are everywhere, nowadays, inspiring kids and adults alike. While you may know Spider-Man best from his cinematic exploits or perhaps his animated series, it's important to note that the source of all things web-head isn't his radioactive blood, it's comic books.

Marvel Comics: Simply Mahvelous, Dahling

In the early years of Marvel Comics, two men by the names of Stan Lee and Jack Kirby would have a huge influence on not only the company they worked for, Marvel Comics, but on comic books in general. Lee and Kirby broke away from the traditional idea of what a superhero was and helped create a *new* type of hero, one who, despite his or her powers, had a core of humanity to which anyone could relate.

We all can understand feeling like a misfit sometimes, and, at its core, that's what the X-Men are about. Stan Lee dreamed up these mutant heroes, in part, to reflect the rampant racial tensions of the 1960s, aiding countless readers to understand what it was like on the other side of the fence.

Spider-Man, Batman, Superman—all single white males. Seeing this tendency for comic book heroes to be in the SWM category, Stan Lee dreamed up a new kind

---

[134] While these books are good, I can't recommend them personally because they're just a bit too brutal and rape-y for my tastes.

[135] An era followed by the Renaissance, and preceded by the Age of Doog, where a man named Doog did pretty much whatever he pleased.

The Top Eleven Greatest Pieces of Fiction-within-Fiction

11 | **Fiction-within-fiction:** *Ow, My Balls*
It's a: show about a dude getting slammed in the balls pretty much non-stop.
Found in: *Idiocracy*

10 | **Fiction-within-fiction:** *All My Circuits*
It's an: all-robot soap opera. Also worth mentioning is *The Scary Door*, a *Twilight Zone* parody.
Found in: *Futurama*

9 | **Fiction-within-fiction:** *Mac and C.H.E.E.S.E.*
It's a: short-lived show about a detective solving crimes with his robot buddy.
Found in: *Friends*

8 | **Fiction-within-fiction:** *Night Springs*
It's a: nod to *The Twilight Zone*, complete with morality tales and Serling-esque narration.
Found in: *Alan Wake*

7 | **Fiction-within-fiction:** *The Steel Samurai*
It's a: Toku show about a dude battling the forces of badness.
Found in: *The Phoenix Wright, Ace Attorney series*

6 | **Fiction-within-fiction:**
Jabberwocky
It's a: nonsensical poem about a brave warrior vanquishing the vile Jabberwock.
Found in: *Through the Looking Glass*

5 | **Fiction-within-fiction:** *Galaxy Quest*
It's a: *Star Trek* knock-off.
Found in: *Galaxy Quest*

4 | **Fiction-within-fiction:** *It's Not My Problem*
It's a: show famous mostly for the catch phrase, *"I'd buy that for a dollar!"*
Found in: *Robocop*

3 | **Fiction-within-fiction:** *Inspector Spacetime*
It's a: Doctor Who parody that, thanks to the internet, kind of took on a life of its own.
Found in: *Community*

2 | **Fiction-within-fiction:** *I Want to be Your Canary*
It's a: play written by Lord Avon, and seems to be the most popular piece of fiction in all of Gaia.
Found in: *Final Fantasy IX*

1 | **Fiction-within-fiction:** *"Ode To A Small Lump Of Green Putty I Found In My Armpit One Midsummer Morning"*
It's a: poem by *Grunthos the Flatulent.*
Found in: *The Hitchhiker's Guide to the Galaxy*

The Fantastic Four's Most Notable Guest Members

Spider-Man, who once tried to join because he was strapped for cash, eventually (and briefly) became a real member and in a snazzy white suit during the Future Foundation storyline.

She-Hulk, who joined after the *Secret Wars* miniseries wrapped up.

Ghost Rider, who mostly just joined so he could park his bike at the Baxter Building whenever he was downtown.

Ernest P. Weebler, who accidentally became a member due to a clerical error.

of superhero team, one that was not only a group of superpowered crime fighters, but a family. Thusly, the Fantastic Four were born, with original members Reed Richards, the stretching scientist, Ben Grimm, the ever-lovin' blue-eyed Thing, Sue Storm, the Invisible Woman, and her brother, Johnny Storm, the hot-headed Human Torch. Since having a team of five or more would render the FF name moot, their roster tends to stay low, and with relatively few additions or subtractions to their team over the years.

Peter Parker

"You know who I am—your friendly neighborhood Spider-Man"

We all may not all know Peter Parker, but we all know a guy like Peter Parker. He's a good dude with a lot to offer the world, but he's frequently down on his luck and down on himself. Stan Lee created Spider-Man, in part, as part of his personal mission to tell different kinds of stories in comic books. However awesome Batman and Wonder Woman might be, readers can't easily identify with an orphaned billionaire or an Amazonian warrior.

Given the ridiculous, mind-blowing international success of Spider-Man as a multimedia hero, it might be difficult to believe that Stan had to *fight* to get ol' web-head into print. Marvel's then-publisher, Martin Goodman, detested the concept of your friendly neighborhood Spider-Man. "He gave me 1,000 reasons why Spider-Man would never work," said Stan. "'Nobody likes spiders, it sounds too much like Superman, and how could a teenager be a superhero?' Then I told him I wanted the character to be a very human guy, someone who makes mistakes, who worries, who gets acne, has trouble with his girlfriend, things like that.' Goodman's reply? 'He's a hero! He's not an average man!' I said, 'No, we make him an average man who happens to have super powers, that's what will make him good.' He told me I was crazy." Of course, once the sales figures for Amazing Fantasy #15, the issue featuring the first appearance of Spider-Man, came in, Mr. Goodman changed his tune immediately, calling in Stan in to discuss the continuation of 'that Spider-Man guy we both liked so much.'"

Ten X-Men Stories That Sound Insane When Explained Out Loud

With groups such as The Justice League of America and the Avengers, you've got disparate backgrounds for each hero, and different sources of their powers. The X-Men, too, are a pretty diverse bunch, although they always have one thing in common: that X-gene. While the source of the X-Peeps' power may be easy to understand, their adventures sometimes aren't. Some storylines make sense, some less so, and some, well, if you discussed them aloud, you'd realize just how insane they sound.

10 | Quintessential '90s girl Jubilee gets turned into a vampire by the son of Dracula.

9 | A fat, spineless blob creature named Mojo kidnaps the X-Men and puts them on a sadistic inter-dimensional reality show.

8 | Professor X's body gets infested by the Brood, who are basically rip-offs of the aliens from *Alien*, and his soul gets permanently implanted into a cloned body.

7 | Nightcrawler, master of teleportation, teleports into a robot's waiting fist, which kills him (for a while).

6 | Jean Grey gets possessed by a powerful cosmic entity known as the Phoenix Force, and, in a string of events befitting the mythological beast for which she's named, Jean dies and gets resurrected repeatedly, with each revival more implausible than the last.

5 | Nightcrawler's father, a teleporting mutant named Azazel, breaks out of Hell so he can get women pregnant, which will help him break out of Hell, which he clearly doesn't need help doing since he can already break out of Hell.

4 | Magneto uses his powers to rip the adamantium metal from Wolverine's bones.

3 | The introduction of Adam the Xtreme, who may possibly be the third Summers brother.

2 | The time Jean Grey got tentacle arms.

1 | Man, pretty much everything having to do with Xorn, a mutant who both was and wasn't Magneto's imposter.

Outside of those uncanny mutants and that fantastic family, The Avengers is one of the most well-known teams of marvel superheroes, *especially* after their film annihilated the box office. The Avengers' roster may have changed a lot over the years, but they've always stuck by their battle cry of "Avengers Assemble!" even if it's been suggested they change it.

DC Comics: Detective Comics Comics

Marvel and DC Comics each have their own approaches to handling story continuity. Since World War II, Marvel has kept their characters roughly within the same line of continuity, which helps readers feel invested, but also makes for a hell of a mess when trying to explain an individual character's history.[136] DC Comics, on the other hand, reboots their continuity every once in a while as a method of clean-up, keeping the bits their editors feel everyone likes and paring away the rest.

Top Five Rejected Avengers Battle Cries and the Avengers Who Suggested Them

5 | RAAAGHLARRRGGHHHUUUUU - The Hulk

4 | To hell with it! - Hawkeye

3 | Hey, can you guys hear me? What's going on up there? - Ant Man

2 | We hold these truths to be self-evident, that all men are created equal, that they are endowed by their Creator with certain unalienable Rights, that among these are Life, Liberty and the pursuit of Happiness. - Captain America

1 | Hold on, I'm getting a text. - Iron Man

---

[136] Think about how many insane adventures, battles, and crises Wolverine has taken part in. When you combine that with the fact that the guy's on like four different teams at any one time, it makes you wonder how in the hell he's got time to have done all of this stuff.

While this can help new readers get invested, it can feel like a slap in the face to older, loyal readers, and makes for an *even* bigger mess when trying to explain to someone that, say, that particular adventure of *The Flash* starred the pre-*Crisis on Infinite Earths* Barry Allen, not the post-*Zero Hour,* post-*Infinite Crisis,* pre-*New 52* Wally West.

Despite DC's proclivity toward reboots and retcons, *Batman*'s backstory always remains largely untouched. There's always a boy, his parents, and a vicious mugger, and it always leads to the same thing—*Batman.*

First-Hand Geekiness: Eleven Reasons We Love Batman

(11) | Created by Bob Kane and Bill Finger in 1939, during the months after Superman exploded onto the scene with all his impossible powers, Batman became the original comic book superhero with*out* superpowers. When we grow old enough to know better than to believe a man can fly, we can still cling to the sense that one man with the right gadgets, skills, and sheer determination could make a difference.

(10) | Batman's origin is tragic and brutally believable. It taps into our most primal fears because everybody learns that sooner or later, their parents can and will die. Even if we've undergone no tragedy like the one that struck Bruce Wayne's family, when a mugger gunned a boy's parents down before the lad's very eyes, we can sympathize with his suffering and we can understand his desire to do something about it. Of all the better-known superhero origin stories, his is the most human in how it begins, in the moment that makes him everything he will be.

(9) | Bruce Wayne builds himself into the kind of man he chooses to be. Learning that no one has superpowers includes learning that you'll never gain them either, and yet Batman shows we can still become better. Bruce Wayne's inheritance and vast resources, while important, are insufficient without his own characteristics, practice, and resolve. No radioactive spider or magic ring made Bruce Wayne a superhero. He turned himself into something fantastic. We'd love to be heroes, so we love this self-made hero.

(8) | We want to stand up to life's bullies. When you're a kid getting pushed around on the playground or you see someone getting mistreated, you wish you were able to

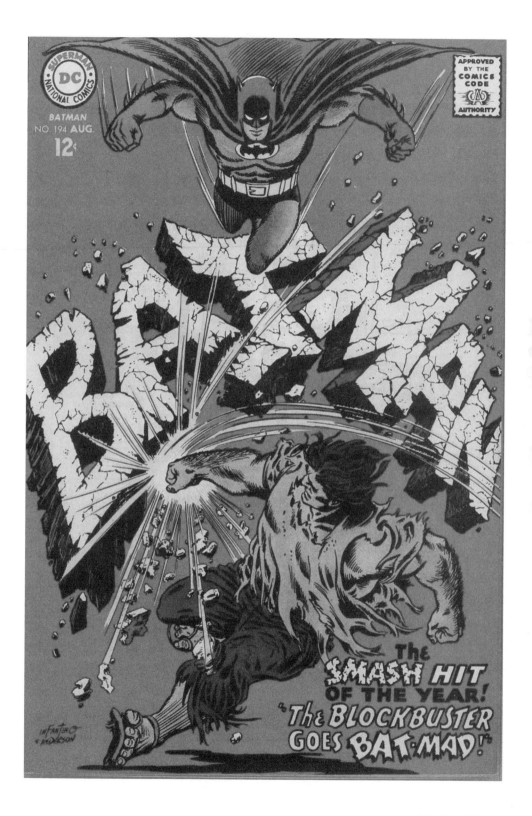

stand up and push back, to make the bullies stop, to teach them a lesson, and maybe to make them feel some of their hurt they've inflicted on others.

(7) | And even if we can't make those bullies stop on our own, we might wish someone else would step in and help. Surely somebody can stop them, can't they? Won't they? We want a Batman to swing onto the scene.

(6) | We want the wicked to feel the kind of fear they instill in others. While Superman flies around in bright blue, inspiring hope, Batman dresses himself in darkness, confident that criminals are a superstitious, cowardly lot who must cower before him.

(5) | Adventure! There's so much more to Batman than darkness and gloom. If there weren't, many other dark heroes over the years might have replaced him as our Dark Knight. No, there's a sense of fun and adventure, moreso in some tales than others.

(4) | We love his car.

(3) | We love his costume.

(2) | We love his crazy foes. His enemies have fun of their own. No other superhero has such a well-known gallery of rogues ready to challenge him and intrigue us. As if they spilled out of the fog one chilly Halloween night, they come to entertain and scare.

(1) | Batman doesn't give up.

– Dr. Travis Langley
Author of *Batman and Psychology: A Dark and Stormy Knight*
@Superherologist

Dr. William Moulton Marston created Wonder Woman to help rectify the lack of admirable female characters in popular culture. "Not even girls want to be girls so long as our feminine archetype lacks force, strength, and power," said Marston. "Not wanting to be girls, they don't want to be tender, submissive, peace-loving as good women are. Women's strong qualities have become despised because of their weakness. The obvious remedy is to create a feminine character with all the strength of Superman plus all the allure of a good and beautiful woman."

In her original backstory, Wonder Woman began her days living on the women-only isle of the Amazons, but when pilot Steve Trevor crashed his plane there, Wonder Woman heard the call to action and returned with him to the U.S. so

GEEK Spotlight

Dr. William Moulton Marston

"Realize what you really want.
It stops you from chasing butterflies and puts you to work digging gold."

The life story of William Moulton Marston is almost as interesting as any of Wonder Woman's superheroic exploits. Not only did he create this iconic superhero, but he also invented the precursor to the polygraph, otherwise known as a lie detector machine. The search for truth seemed to be a dominant theme in Marston's ideology—hence Wonder Woman's signature Lasso of Truth. Marston's contribution to both comic books and feminism are enormous; without Wonder Woman to lead the way, later leading ladies like Buffy the Vampire Slayer, Sarah Connor, and several of the X-Men may not have come around.

Oh, and fun fact: Marston was fairly non-traditional in his sexual exploits. Dude was mad into bondage, and spent his latter years in a marriage a trois with Elizabeth Holloway Marston and Olive Byrne, both of whom heavily influenced the inception of Wonder Woman. After Marston passed away, Olive and Elizabeth spent the remainder of their lives together.

Top Five of the Weirdest Batman, Superman, and Superman/Batman Covers

Batman's bat-family has had more than a few members over the years, what with all the different Robins, Batgirls, and Batwomen who fight the good fight in Gotham City, but one of his most oddly compelling friendships is with the Man of Steel himself, Superman, which is why there've been so many stories featuring the two characters together ... although some of those stories have ended up being a little weirder than you'd expect.

5 | *Detective Comics # 241.* Batman, apparently stricken with obsessive-compulsive disorder, must wear a different-colored Batman uniform every night he goes out on patrol. The cover features him in a shocking pink number.

4 | *Superman's Pal, Jimmy Olsen # 30.* This one's weird on a lot of levels. First off is the fact that Jimmy Olsen is giving Superman a gift, and the box is labeled *To Dad Superman* because Superman has inexplicably adopted Jimmy as his son. Second of all is the fact that Superman is using his heat vision to *torch* the friggin' thing because he says it'll teach Jimmy a lesson.

3 | *Batman #191.* Batman's gone broke, and he's sick of fighting crime, so he's selling everything in the bat-cave, costumes included!

2 | *World's Finest #54.* Batman, Superman, and Robin are all riding a three-man tandem bike. Batman and Supes are kicking back and relaxing like total *jerks* while Robin pedals his little heart out.

1 | *World's Finest #195.* Batman and Superman force Robin and Jimmy Olsen to dig the boys' own graves. Batman has a tommy gun in hand, and Superman's busy explaining that, while *he* has a code against killing them, Batman has no problem gunning the two sidekicks down as soon as they're done digging.

she could help in the fight against the Nazis. DC has fudged this backstory a bit since then, given that it would make Wonder Woman nearly a hundred if it were still the case, but her core of strength and compassion has always remained the same.

Her character seems ripe for a multimedia adaptation, but Joss Whedon's too wrapped up in *The Avengers* and DC seems too scared to make a move with anyone who isn't Batman or Superman. Whenever they do gather the courage to adapt their characters to film or television, they keep trusting the wrong people to do it, evidenced by the very poor *Green Lantern* film and the abysmal, Thank-God-it-never-aired *Wonder Woman* television pilot by Ally McBeal creator David E. Kelley, a pilot that took the strong, moral Wonder Woman and made her into a thug-slaying whine bag who takes solace in ice cream and the fact that she only has a single Facebook friend—her cat.

Barry Allen

"Hey, kid. Name's The Flash, nice to meet ya."

On the *Lost* episode "Catch-22," Hurley and Charlie argue who would win in a race—Superman or the Flash. Silly boys, this question is so easy to answer it shouldn't even have to be answered. The Flash is the Fastest Man Alive. Every superpowered thing he can do stems from his ability to manipulate the Speed Force and get wacky with the physical laws of the universe. Of *course* he'd win a race against Superman. Superman can run, skip, or fly, but The Flash is faster because *he's the freaking Flash.*

Many men have held the title of the Flash, but (currently) only Barry Allen can lay claim to being the fastest man alive.[137] Barry's a forensic scientist famous for taking his time with his lab work and being late to everything—which later becomes a ploy to cover up his secret identity. While most heroes have a grim and gritty phase somewhere in their history, Barry's time as the Flash is usually about as bright as it gets. He's upbeat and superheroic, inspiring other heroes to remember the good even when it gets bad. Batman describes Barry as "the kind of man I hope I would have been had my parents not been murdered."

He's also pretty much the only superhero for whom death was a major detriment. After his noble sacrifice during Crisis on Infinite Earth, Barry stayed dead for over *twenty* years, a stunningly long absence for such a popular character.

---

[137] Or dead, given that Barry outran death itself.

Other Notable Superhero Deaths
(and How Long They Stayed Dead)

BATMAN

Cause of death: Laser beam from Darkseid.

Length of death: Approximately one year, real time.

Reason he wasn't really dead: Darkseid's laser didn't actually kill him, it sent him through time.

COLOSSUS

Cause of death: Self-sacrifice to create a cure for the Legacy Virus.

Length of death: Approximately two years, comic time.

Reason he wasn't really dead: An alien named Ord swapped Colossus' body with a duplicate and then resuscitated him while the dupe got cremated.

THE HUMAN TORCH

Cause of death: Horde of aliens from The Negative Zone.

Length of death: Approximately two years, comic time.

Reason he came back: Annihilus implanted little bugs in his body that revived him.

CAPTAIN AMERICA

Cause of death: Crossbones shoots him with a sniper rifle, and Dr. Faustus uses hypnosis to command Sharon Carter to shoot Cap to finish him off.

Length of death: Approximately two years, real time.

Reason he wasn't really dead: The gun didn't kill Cap, it caused him to go out of sync with space and time. (See the death of Batman, above.)

SUPERMAN

Cause of death: Beaten to death by Doomsday, a huge rock dude invented (by the writers) for the sole purpose of slaying Superman.

Length of death: Approximately two years, real time.

Reason he wasn't really dead: Superman never died, he dropped into a Kryptonian coma so that, with a little help from the Fortress of Solitude, his body could heal from the savage beating he was dealt.

LIGHTNING LAD

Cause of death: Self-sacrifice during a battle with Zaryan the Conqueror.

Length of death: A couple of months, real time.

Reason he came back: Proty, Chameleon Boy's shapeshifting pet, sacrifices himself to revive Lightning Lad.

PROFESSOR X

Causes of deaths: (1) Explosion. **(2)** Brood egg implantation. **(3)** Stryfe shot him with a bullet infected with a techno-virus. **(4)** Accidentally shot by Bishop. **(5)** Cyclops, possessed by the Phoenix Force, kills him.

Length of deaths: Varies wildly.

Reason he wasn't really dead/reason he came back:

(1) The explosion actually blew up Changeling *disguised* as the Professor, not the *real* Professor. **(2)** His mind was transferred into a cloned body. **(3)** Apocalypse did his Apocalypse-y thing. **(4)** Exodus and Omega Sentinel did their Exodus and Omega Sentinel things. **(5)** As of this writing he has yet to return from this death, but you'd be smart to keep the seat on his wheelchair warm for him, because he probably won't be gone for long.

GREEN LANTERN (HAL JORDAN)

Cause of death: Gets infected by Parallax, the cosmic embodiment of fear, and does a bunch of bad stuff before coming to his senses and heroically sacrificing himself to undo some of the badness that had happened.

Length of death: Approximately ten years, real time.

Reason he came back: A whole mess of stuff involving the Guardians, power rings, Parallax, and Geoff Johns writing his way out of the dead end previous writers had left Hal in.

Hal Jordan

"In brightest day, in blackest night ..."

The Green Lanterns are among the most powerful superheroes around, given that their rings can generate constructs based on the imagination and will power of their wielder, and yet writers consistently find a way to keep these ultra-powered guys *human.* Alan Scott's a dad.[138] Kyle Rayner is chillaxed and imaginative. John Stewart's a military man. Guy Gardner is a hot-headed ass-kicker. And the way they made Hal Jordan relatable? By making him *friggin' awesome.*

Green Lantern Hal Jordan and Barry Allen, a.k.a. the Flash, are superhero BFFs. Together they're sort of like bad cop and good cop, with Hal being more prone to flying off the handle and Barry keeping his cool. Barry has to keep his cool to keep his powers under control—since he taps into the Speed Force, it'd be easy for him to go ballistic and end up spaghettified across time and space. And Hal may be a little hard-headed—okay, so he's *really* hard-headed—but his powers are based on sheer force of will, so a little stubbornness goes with that, you know? Plus, unlike many other heroes, Hal's had to deal with a number of weaknesses over the years, and he needs every bit of willpower he can get to not succumb to them.

---

[138] It should be pointed out that Green Lantern Alan Scott has no direct relation to the Green Lantern Corps to which the other Green Lanterns belong, they just have the same name. It should also be pointed out that goofy stuff like that is why non-comic book fans look at us all cross-eyed when we try to explain characters and storylines to them.

Twelve Things Most Green Lanterns Wouldn't Admit Their Rings Are Weak Against

12 | The color yellow

11 | Wood[139]

10 | Salted bass

9 | Sam Malone from *Cheers*

8 | Chinchillas

7 | Roald Dahl books

6 | Magic the Gathering's Black Lotus card

5 | Those who would dare pronounce the word "Library" as "Liberry"

4 | Any academic paper containing the word heteroskedasticity.

3 | Weasels

2 | Prime numbers

1 | Steve Buscemi

[139] #12 and #11 are actual, real weaknesses the Green Lanterns have had at times.

Those Proud Few: Independent Comic Books

Though Marvel and DC Comics may make up a significant share of comic book sales, there are plenty of other worthwhile titles out there from plenty of other worthwhile publishers.

The *Scott Pilgrim* graphic novel series achieved impressive success thanks, in no small part, to its manic mixture of romantic comedy tropes and anime-inspired storylines and brawls. Our hero, Scott Pilgrim, is kind of an ass—whiny, unemployed, and *self-involved* ass—but when he hooks up with the mysterious and more grown-up Ramona Flowers, her evil ex-boyfriends come a-knockin', forcing him to get with the program and man up if he hopes to hang onto his lady love. The *Scott Pilgrim* story is a love letter to video games while also drawing inspiration from the Manga comics of the Far East and converting them to a format more palatable to the mass Western market. The success of the comic series also led to a movie, *Scott Pilgrim vs. the World*, which may not have been a blockbuster success, but did a fan-freaking-tastic job of adapting the fun of the comic book story to the big screen.

If you're like me, you've watched your share of horror movies and gotten annoyed at how incompetent many characters are, particularly those poor gals whose job it is to get killed the opening scene. When Joss Whedon created Buffy the Vampire Slayer, he did so out of wondering what it would be like if the "first girl" being hunted by the movie's monster turned around and kicked that monster's ass. *Hack/Slash* took that same bit of inspiration and ran with it. Hero Cassandra Hack and her partner, the hulking Vlad, traverse the country looking for Slashers, undead marauders and murderers who enjoy cutting up those who are young-of-flesh and short-of-brains. Eventually the comic settles into having an over-arcing storyline, but for much of its run it's about Vlad and Cassie essentially stumbling into slasher movie after slasher movie and putting an end to things before the body counts get too high. Cassie's a funny, tough, and lonely chick, one who draws you back issue after issue. Sometimes the art suffers from an over-emphasis on Male Gaze, but the comic's so much damn fun that minor annoyances like that don't really matter.

Another horror comic that's definitely less fun than *Hack/Slash* would be *The Walking Dead*. If given the option to live in a comic book's universe, I hope that you'd pick anything other than the universe of *The Walking Dead*, because it's an awful place. There are zombies everywhere, and psychotic, one-eyed governors doing all sorts of evil things. Even the good guys get so beat down by the brutality of life that it's hard for them to stay *that* good. It's one gripping comic, though, and it has made for an equally gripping television show.

If you're a fan of comic books which lie outside the beaten path, why not also check out: *Hellboy, Sandman, Atomic Robo, Y: the Last Man, Locke and Key, Milk and Cheese,* and *The Teenage Mutant Ninja Turtles.*

Newspaper Comics: They Still Make Newspapers, Don't They?

Sonny, it may surprise you to know that newspapers used to be the way we got information around. What's a newspaper, you ask? Well, it's a pile of smudgy papers produced weekly, or sometimes daily, filled with the latest information about business, the arts, and the world in general. Yeah, those were simpler times. *Slower* times, where people sometimes didn't find out about big world events until hours, sometimes even *days* after it happened.

To some, newspapers can seem like they're dumb, old, and dying. As Egon Spengler stated so eloquently, "Print is dead." It might not be long before traditional newspapers get phased out entirely, but no matter their fate, they can rest easy knowing they contributed some amazing comics (that we hope somehow survive).[140]

PEARLS BEFORE SWINE

Creator: Stephan Pastis
Main characters: Pig, Rat, Zebra, and Goat
What it's about: Cute characters and surprisingly dark jokes (for a newspaper comic).
Notable moment: Two alligators, in an attempt to intimidate their zebra neighbor, mime Popeye the sailor man, with one humming his theme song and the other, squinty-eyed gator swallowing the contents of a can of spinach. Popeyegator swiftly chokes and dies. After an elongated silence, his partner proclaims, "Today's lesson: Always chew you food."

DILBERT

Creator: Scott Adams
Main characters: Dilbert, Dogbert, Wally, Alice, Asok, and the Pointy-Haired Boss.
What it's about: Corporate life.[141]
Notable moment: Phil, the Prince of Insufficient Light and ruler of Heck, darns Dilbert to sitting in the secretary's chair for a day to endure the banal jokes of his coworkers.

---

[140] There are far too many interesting, geeky newspaper comics out there for this book to list them all, so if you're wondering where *Family Circus* is, it's not here because 1. I only have so much room to write, and 2. *Family Circus* blows.

[141] I read a ton of comics when I was ~10, with this one being in more heavy rotation. Going back through my old *Dilbert* books, I don't understand why the hell I read it so much—it's not like I could relate to any of the jokes about corporate life in the new millennium.

Calvin and Hobbes

Calvin: *"They say the world is a stage. But obviously the play is unrehearsed and everybody is ad-libbing his lines."*

Hobbes: *"Maybe that's why it's hard to tell if we're living in a tragedy or a farce."*

Calvin: *"We need more special effects and dance numbers."*

Being a smart kid isn't all that it's cracked up to be. You'll spend most of your days in school bored out of your mind by being subjected to material that's far below your cognitive level, surrounded by kids you can't identify with. With *Calvin and Hobbes,* however, the smartypantses found someone who understood what we were feeling. Like us, here was a kid who was a little too smart and a little too weird for his own good. Alongside him is his tiger buddy, Hobbes, who some claim to be an imaginary friend.[142]

Hobbes may be a tiger, but that doesn't mean he lacks thoughtfulness. He's Calvin's faithful bud, but he's also the first to offer a word of warning when Calvin's idea-of-the-day seems less than sensible. Together they explored the magical world around them, encountering weirdos from Mars, surviving the thing drooling under the bed, all while making sense of the craziness of life, girls, and growing up. Calvin and Hobbes' creator, Bill Watterson, retired from the comic when he was still at the top of his game, and though the lack of C&H is felt every single day, their contribution to the world still holds strong.

---

[142] I like to think of Hobbes more like Ludo, Hoggle, and Sir Didymus from *Labyrinth*: they may not appear to the mundanes, but that doesn't mean they're not real.

PEANUTS

Creator: Charles Schultz

What it's about: A bald kid and his group of friends.

Notable moment: When Charlie Brown tried to kick the football and that mean-ass Lucy removes it at the last moment, leaving him flat on his back. Then Charlie Brown calmly gets up and makes Lucy eat the football.[143]

GARFIELD

Creator: Jim Davis

Main characters/What it's about: A mundane man named Jon Arbuckle, his dopey dog Odie, and Garfield, a fat cat who loves lasagna, hates spiders, and can't stand Mondays.

Notable moment: In 1989, one storyline saw Garfield waking up to an empty, decrepit house, one that's clearly been abandoned for years. Unable to cope with his loneliness, Garfield has a fit of rage/sadness/sheer willpower and returns to his home... although the final box of narration implies that *this* may be the imagined reality, and that Garfield may actually be a crazy cat living in a house alone.

FUNKY WINKERBEAN: DARKNESS UNBOUND[144]

Creator: Tom Batiuk

Main characters: Les Moore, Funky Winkerbean, and a bunch of other equally downtrodden suburbanites.

What it's about: Miserable people counting down the seconds until they die. They also deal with things such as suicide, child abuse, cancer, death, post-traumatic stress disorder, and a whole bunch of other topics which really put the "funny" in the "funny pages."

Notable moment: If it seems as if I'm painting a dark picture of *Funky Winkerbean,* it's because the comic seems to revel in nihilism and depression. Chris Sims of ComicsAlliance.com wrote a hilarious series of articles highlighting the most depressing Funky Winkerbean comics of each month. You'd think that he'd run out of ammunition to do a monthly column, and yet, month after month, Tom Batiuk would churn out comics that were blacker than the blackest night, giving those with a morbid sense of humor (like yours truly) a good laugh and prompting everyone else to wonder whether Mr. Batiuk was feeling okay. Tom, if you're reading this, you're a good person, and life is for the living.

While most newspaper comics are famous for making their homes there, there are a few surprising comics originating from other media which have graced the funny pages on a daily/weekly basis, such as: *The Amazing Spider-Man, Batman and Robin, Wonder*

---

[143] Okay, so that last part didn't really happen. But don't you wish it did?

[144] All right, it's really just *Funky Winkerbean*, but given the comic's soul-crushing contents, it might as well be called that.

Woman, Howard the Duck, Popeye, The Teenage Mutant Ninja Turtles, Felix the Cat, Buck Rogers, The Phantom, Rugrats, Star Trek, Star Wars, Bugs Bunny, and *Boner's Ark*, which I only included in this list because the name is too hilarious not to.

Gary Larson

"This was more than just a cow — this was an entire career I was looking at."

Few artists and authors manage to capture the existential weirdness of simply *being* as brilliantly as Gary Larson did during his days of writing *The Far Side*. This frequently bizarre, always genius, comic held a funhouse mirror up to humanity and showed us that, nope, *we're* the ones who are twisted, and our reflections are what's normal. In the syndicated comic strip, we saw things like a class full of white-belt level martial arts students preparing to save the Earth from an invading force of brick-bodies, board-limbed aliens. In another comic, a chicken husband bemoans his chicken wife feeding him chicken soup to help him recover from the flu. And the truth behind dinosaur extinction? The dummies just wouldn't quit smoking.

Larson's ability to anthropomorphize objects, animals, and concepts is one of his many charms. So many of his comics hit their subjects from such a beautifully bizarre angle that it'll make you slap your face and curse yourself for not thinking of it first.

Epilogue:
I Dream of Electric Sheep
Also, of Spider-Man Giving Me a Chemistry Test While I'm Naked

If you've been reading this book,[145] you've noticed that it covers quite the bevy of topics. We've scoured the history of geeky television; we've talked about the magic of long-form storytelling and the tragic brevity of some of geekdom's favorite shows; we examined geeky movies of all kinds, from the smallest of budgets to the biggest of box-office spectacles. We also read up on geeky books, pressed start on geeky video games, logged onto the internet, and even checked out a few scientists— the original geeks. While these topics are as diverse as they are awesome, one thing unites them: passion. Being a geek isn't about what we love as much as it's about how we love it. We geeks love with a fiery passion, like gasoline-soaked lovers standing too close to an open flame. With all of the topics discussed in this book there are geeky levels of zeal on both sides. The people behind our favorite stories, hobbies, and research all poured themselves into the topics they loved in that obsessive, brilliant, raw way that only we geeks can. And, on the flip side, those of us absorbing those stories, enjoying those hobbies, and using that research to conduct our own research are happy to lose ourselves in it. Whether you're a lifelong geek or considering cosplaying for the first time, revel in your geekery, in your passion to do what you do, and for frak's sake, never stop doing it.

---

[145] And if you haven't been reading this book, what are you doing reading the end? Cheater!

Photo Credits

P. 5: Clockwise from top: *Battlestar Galactica* cast–NBC Universal Television/David Eick Productions; Marie Curie–Wikimedia Commons/public domain; Wonder Woman (Linda Carter)–Warner Bros. Television/Heritage Auctions; *Eureka*'s Henry Deacon (Joe Morton)–Syfy/NBC Universal Television.

P. 7: Clockwise from top: Godzilla–Toho/Heritage Auctions; Xena (Lucy Lawless)–Renaissance Pictures; *Batman: The Animated Series*–DC Comics/Warner Bros. Animation/Warner Bros. Television.

P. 11: *The Walking Dead* comic book–Robert Kirkman/Tony Moore/Image Comics; *Spirited Away* movie poster–Studio Ghibli/Toho/Heritage Auctions; the *Ghostbusters* gang–Columbia Pictures/Heritage Auctions.

P. 12: Dr. Albert Einstein–AP Photo.

P. 16 and 17: Marvel Comics–Heritage Auctions.

P. 18: *The Six Million Dollar Man*'s Steve Austin (Lee Majors)–Harve Bennett Productions/Heritage Auctions.

P. 19: *Star Trek: The Next Generation*'s Data (Brent Spiner)–Paramount Television.

P. 22: Movie still from *The Matrix*–Warner Bros./Heritage Auctions.

P. 25: Movie still from *Ghostbusters*–Columbia Pictures/Heritage Auctions.

P. 26: *Big Foot* movie poster–Ellman Enterprises/Heritage Auctions.

P. 27: Bartlesville: Porterhouse/Heritage Auctions.

P. 30: Archimedes–Wikimedia Commons/public domain.

P. 31: Tesla–Heritage Auctions; Gutenberg–Wikimedia Commons/public domain.

P. 32: Carver–Wikimedia Commons/public domain; Da Vinci–AP Photo; Mendel–Wikimedia Commons/public domain.

P. 33: Darwin–Heritage Auctions; Linnaeus–Wikimedia Commons/public domain.

P. 34: Galileo–Wikimedia Commons/public domain; Curie–Wikimedia Commons/public domain; Freud–AP Photo.

P. 35: Einstein–Heritage Auctions; Franklin–Wikimedia Commons/public domain.

P. 36: *Star Trek*'s Spock (Leonard Nimoy) and Captain Kirk (William Shatner)–Paramount Television/Heritage Auctions.

P. 39: *Buffy the Vampire Slayer* cast–Mutant Enemy/20th Century Fox Television.

P. 40: *Buffy*'s Willow (Alyson Hannigan)–Mutant Enemy/20th Century Fox Television.

P. 43: Sokku–Nickelodeon Animation Studios.

P. 44: Edward Scissorhands (Johnny Depp)–20th Century Fox/Heritage Auctions.

P. 46: *The Lion King*'s Simba–Disney/Heritage Auctions.

P. 47: *Game of Thrones* promotional poster–Home Box Office (HBO).

P. 48: The Wicked Witch (Margaret Hamilton) from *The Wizard of Oz*–Metro-Goldwyn-Mayer/Heritage Auctions.

P. 50: *300* movie poster–Warner Bros./Heritage Auctions; Bela Lugosi's Dracula–Universal Pictures/Heritage Auctions.

P. 51: *Supernatural*'s Sam and Dean Winchester–Warner Bros. Television.

P. 52: *The Walking Dead*'s Daryl Dixon (Norman Reedus)–American Movie Classics.

P. 53: A still from *The Walking Dead*–American Movie Classics; *Cowboy Bebop*'s Spike Spiegel/Bandai Visual Co.; Sarah Connor (Lena Headey) from *Terminator: The Sarah Connor Chronicles*–Warner Bros. Television/20th Century Fox Television.

P. 55: *True Blood*'s Lafayette (Nelsan Ellis)–Home Box Office (HBO).

P. 56: *Star Trek*'s Captain Kirk (William Shatner)–Paramount Television/Heritage Auctions.

P. 62: *Firefly*'s Captain Malcolm Reynolds (Nathan Fillion)–Mutant Enemy/20th Century Fox Television.

P. 63: *Firefly* cast–Mutant Enemy/20th Century Fox Television.

P. 65: *Doctor Who*–British Broadcasting Corp. (BBC).

P. 67: *DuckTale*'s Gyro Gearloose–Walt Disney Television Animation.

P. 68: *Scooby Doo*'s Velma–Hanna-Barbera Productions.

P. 71: *Warehouse 13*'s Claudia Donovan (Allison Scagliotti)–Syfy/Universal Cable Productions; *The Big Bang Theory*'s Sheldon Cooper (Jim Parsons)–CBS/Chuck Lorre Productions/Warner Bros. Television; *Community*'s Abed Nadir (Danny Pudi)–NBC/Sony Pictures Television.

P. 72: *Dragon Ball Z*–FUNimation Entertainment/Toei Animation Company.

P. 74: *Pokémon*–Pokémon USA; *The Golden Girls*–Touchstone Television/Heritage Auctions.

P. 75: *Ghost in the Shell*'s Major Motoko Kusanagi–Bandai Visual Company.

P. 76: *The Incredible Hulk*'s Dr. David Banner (Bill Bixby)–Universal TV/Heritage Auctions.

P. 77: DC Comics/Heritage Auctions.

P. 78: *Eureka*'s Douglas Fargo (Neil Grayston)–Syfy/NBC Universal Television.

P. 79: *The X-Files*–20th Century Fox Television/Heritage Auctions.

P. 82: *Family Matters*–Lorimar Television/Warner Bros. Television.

P. 83: Urkel (Jaleel White)–Lorimar Television/Warner Bros. Television.

P. 84: Bill Cosby–Casey-Werner Co./NBC.

P. 85: *Ghostbusters* movie poster–Columbia Pictures/Heritage Auctions.

P. 89: *Batman*'s Batman (Michael Keaton) and The Joker (Jack Nicholson)–Warner Bros./DC Comics/Heritage Auctions.

P. 90: *Batman and Robin*'s Poison Ivy (Uma Thurman) and Mr. Freeze (Arnold Schwarzenegger)–Warner Bros./DC Comics/Heritage Auctions.

P. 91: Iron Man (Robert Downey Jr.)–Paramount Pictures/Marvel Enterprises.

P. 93: *Independence Day*'s Captain Steven Hiller (Will Smith)–20th Century Fox.
P. 94: *Men in Black* movie poster–Columbia Pictures/Heritage Auctions.
P. 95: Darth Vader–Lucasfilm/20th Century Fox/Heritage Auctions.
P. 96: Chewbacca and Han Solo–Lucasfilm/20th Century Fox/Heritage Auctions.
P. 97: Ben Kenobi–Lucasfilm/20th Century Fox/Heritage Auctions.
P. 98: *Alien* museum poster–20th Century Fox/Heritage Auctions.
P. 99: *The Thing*'s R.J. MacReady (Kurt Russell)–Universal Pictures/Heritage Auctions; *Predator*'s Dutch (Arnold Schwarzenegger)–20th Century Fox/Heritage Auctions.
P. 101: Dr. Ian Malcolm (Jeff Goldblum)–Universal Pictures/Heritage Auctions.
P. 103: Still photos from *Terminator 2: Judgment Day*–Tri-Star/Heritage Auctions.
P. 106: *I, Robot*–20th Century Fox/Heritage Auctions.
P. 108: *Jiro Dreams of Sushi* movie poster–Sundial Pictures.
P. 110: A movie still from *King Kong*–RKO/Heritage Auctions.
P. 111: A gremlin and a mogwai–Warner Bros.
P. 112: *Poltergeist*'s Carol Anne (Heather O'Rourke)–MGM/UA/Heritage Auctions.
P. 114: *Troll 2*–Filmirage.
P. 115: *Back to the Future*'s Doc Brown (Christopher Lloyd) and Marty (Michael J. Fox) – Universal/Heritage Auctions.
P. 116: *Groundhog Day* movie poster–Columbia/Heritage Auctions.
P. 117: *Hook*'s Rufio (Dante Basco)–Tri-Star.
P. 118: Hayao Miyazaki–AP Photo/Joel Ryan.
P. 120: *Dawn of the Dead* poster book–United Film Distribution/Heritage Auctions.
P. 121: Conan (Arnold Schwarzenegger)–Universal/Heritage Auctions; Mad Max (Mel Gibson)–Warner Bros./Heritage Auctions.
P. 122: A still from *Night of the Living Dead*–Continental/Heritage Auctions.

P. 124: Three Rivers press.
P. 125: *Speed Racer* movie poster–Warner Bros./Heritage Auctions; *The Last Airbender* movie poster–Paramount Pictures.
P. 127: *Planet of the Apes* movie poster–20th Century Fox/Heritage Auctions.
P. 128: Warhammer space marine soldier–Hot Property/Shutterstock.
P. 132: *Mass Effect*–BioWare/Microsoft Game Studios/Electronic Arts.
P. 133: *Mass Effect*'s Tali–BioWare/Microsoft Game Studios/Electronic Arts.
P. 135: *Super Mario Bros.*' Mario–Nintendo/Shigeru Miyamoto.
P. 137: Mega Man–Capcom.
P. 140: *Super Metroid*–Nintendo/Makoto Kano.
P. 141: Sonic the Hedgehog–Sega.
P. 143: *Chrono Trigger*'s Luca Ashtear–Square Enix/Kazuhiko Aoki.
P. 150: *Ultimate Mortal Kombat 3*–Midway Games.
P. 151: *E.T. The Extra-Terrestrial*–Atari.
P. 152: *Grand Theft Auto III*–DMA Design/Rockstar Games/Capcom.
P. 154: *Resident Evil 2*–Capcom.
P. 160: Nathan Drake–Naughty Dog/Sony Computer Entertainment; Solid Snake–Konami/Microsoft Game Studios.
P. 161: Bayonetta–Platinum Games/Sega.
P. 162: Cloud Strife–Square Enix.
P. 164: Unsuspecting cat surfing the internet–Hasloo Production Studio/Shutterstock.
P. 172: Katrina Hill–Jennifer Kelley Lublin.
P. 175: Felicia Day–AP Photo/Matt Sayles.
P. 176: Chris Hardwick–AP Photo/Shea Walsh.
P. 184: First edition *The Hitchhikers Guide to the Galaxy*–Arthur Barker Limited/Heritage Auctions.
P. 186: *Alice in Wonderland*–Winston/Heritage Auctions; *The Wonderful Wizard of Oz*–George M. Hill Company/Heritage Auctions.
P. 187: *The Lord of the Rings*–Houghton Mifflin Company/Heritage Auctions.

P. 189: *The War of the Worlds*–Looking Glass Library/Heritage Auctions.
P. 190: *Frankenstein*–George Routledge and Sons/Heritage Auctions.
P. 192: *It*–Warner Bros. Television.
P. 194: Framed portrait of Edgar Allen Poe–Heritage Auctions.
P. 197: *The Colour of Magic*–St. Martin's Press/Heritage Auctions.
P. 198: *Harry Potter and the Philosopher's Stone*–Bloombury/Heritage Auctions.
P. 200: *Harry Potter*'s Hermione Granger–Warner Bros.
P. 202: *The Hunger Games*–Scholastic Press./Heritage Auctions.
P. 204: Rod Serling–Heritage Auctions.
P. 205: *Galaxy Quest*–DreamWorks/Heritage Auctions.
P. 206: *Fantastic Four*–Marvel Comics/Heritage Auctions; *Justice League of America*–DC Comics/Heritage Auctions.
P. 207: Peter Parker/Spider-Man original sketch–Joe Sinnott/Heritage Auctions.
P. 208: *The X-Men*–Marvel Comics/Heritage Auctions.
P. 211: *The Astonishing Ant-Man*–Marvel Comics/Heritage Auctions.
P. 213: *Batman*–DC Comics/Heritage Auctions.
P. 216 and 217: DC Comics/Heritage Auctions.
P. 218: *Wonder Woman*–DC Comics/Heritage Auctions.
P. 219: The Flash–DC Comics.
P. 220-221: Marvel Comics/Heritage Auctions.
P. 223: *Green Lantern*–DC Comics/Heritage Auctions.
P. 224: Sam Malone–Paramount Network Television; *My Uncle Oswald*–Michael Joseph/Heritage Auctions.
P. 227: *Calvin and Hobbes*–Bill Watterson/Universal Press Syndicate/Heritage Auctions.
P. 229: Gary Larson–AP Photo/Tom Reed.

Index

Get your geek on

the geek handbook

Practical Skills and Advice for the Likeable Modern Geek

Alex Langley

In **The Geek Handbook**, author Alex Langley draws on his own knowledge of being a geek for almost 30 years and provides essential advice for growth and survival for the modern geek, including basics on social interaction, fashion, and making friends, dinner, and

ks.com,

your c needs.

Wheth ting for

years, se and

main

You' site and

we e

Be s scounts!

nline

a m - 5 pm CST)

llers

Visit K for everyone

er®